RAND GULF STATES POLICY INSTITUTE

Strengthening Coastal Planning

How Coastal Regions Could Benefit from Louisiana's Planning and Analysis Framework

David G. Groves, Jordan R. Fischbach, Debra Knopman,
David R. Johnson, Kate Giglio

T0308356

This volume was prepared as part of the RAND-Initiated Research program and was funded by the generosity of RAND's donors and by fees earned on client-funded research.

Library of Congress Control Number: 2014933035

ISBN: 978-0-8330-8455-2

The RAND Corporation is a nonprofit institution that helps improve policy and decisionmaking through research and analysis. RAND's publications do not necessarily reflect the opinions of its research clients and sponsors.

Support RAND—make a tax-deductible charitable contribution at www.rand.org/giving/contribute.html

RAND® is a registered trademark.

Cover image: The Inner Harbor Navigation Canal Surge Barrier, developed by the U.S. Army Corps of Engineers after the 2005 hurricane season and completed in 2011, is designed to reduce the risk of storm surge flooding to many parts of New Orleans. It is located to the east of New Orleans and is currently the largest such barrier in the United States. (USACE photo by Paul Floro.)

RAND OFFICES
SANTA MONICA, CA • WASHINGTON, DC
PITTSBURGH, PA • NEW ORLEANS, LA • JACKSON, MS • BOSTON, MA
CAMBRIDGE, UK • BRUSSELS, BE
www.rand.org

Preface

Like many coastal regions, Louisiana faces significant risks from storms and resulting storm surge and flooding, as well as coastal land loss. Furthermore, these risks are likely to be exacerbated by continued development and climate change. Louisiana's Coastal Protection and Restoration Authority (CPRA) took a major step forward to confront these risks in its groundbreaking 2012 report, *Louisiana's Comprehensive Master Plan for a Sustainable Coast,* a 50-year, $50 billion coast-wide strategy for reducing flood risk and coastal land loss. RAND researchers supported CPRA's efforts by developing (1) a structured and analytical approach to support CPRA's decisionmaking, called the Planning Tool, and (2) a computer simulation model of coastal conditions to estimate property and other damages associated with storm surge and flooding, called the Coastal Louisiana Risk Assessment (CLARA) model.

This report highlights RAND's contributions to CPRA's Master Plan, with the goal of helping policymakers in other coastal regions understand the value of a solid technical foundation to support decisionmaking on strategies to reduce flood risks, rebuild or restore coastal environments, and increase the resilience of developed coastlines. It brings together and makes accessible previously published RAND technical descriptions of both the Planning Tool and the CLARA model.

Like Louisiana, other coastal states and their communities are facing the need to rethink and redesign current policy approaches to deal with increasing risk and other coastal planning challenges. And like Louisiana policymakers, many leaders are faced with the task of weighing multiple strategies while faced with substantial uncertainty about how coastal conditions will unfold in the future. This report is intended to serve as a guide to foster new conversations among policymakers, stakeholders, and residents concerned with the well-being of coastal regions across the United States. The planning approach described in this report offers a way to compare many options in a rigorous manner while accounting for a wide range of future uncertainties, including those emerging from a changing climate.

This volume was prepared as part of our RAND-Initiated Research program and was funded by the generosity of RAND's donors and by fees earned on client-funded research. The original research behind this work was sponsored by CPRA and documented in *Planning Tool to Support Louisiana's Decisionmaking on Coastal Protection and Restoration: Technical Description,* by David G. Groves, Christopher Sharon, and Debra Knopman, TR-1266-CPRA, 2012; and *Coastal Louisiana Risk Assessment Model: Technical Description and 2012 Coastal Master Plan Analysis Results,* by Jordan R. Fischbach, David R. Johnson, David S. Ortiz, Benjamin P. Bryant, Matthew Hoover, and Jordan Ostwald, TR-1259-CPRA, 2012.

The RAND Environment, Energy, and Economic Development Program

The research reported here was conducted in the RAND Environment, Energy, and Economic Development Program, which addresses topics relating to environmental quality and regulation, water and energy resources and systems, climate, natural hazards and disasters, and economic development, both domestically and internationally. Program research is supported by government agencies, foundations, and the private sector.

This program is part of RAND Justice, Infrastructure, and Environment, a division of the RAND Corporation dedicated to improving policy and decisionmaking in a wide range of policy domains, including civil and criminal justice, infrastructure protection and homeland security, transportation and energy policy, and environmental and natural resource policy.

Questions or comments about this report should be sent to the project leaders, David Groves (David_Groves@rand.org) or Jordan Fischbach (Jordan_Fischbach@rand.org). For more information about the Environment, Energy, and Economic Development Program, see http://www.rand.org/energy or contact the director at eeed@rand.org.

RAND Gulf States Policy Institute

RAND created the Gulf States Policy Institute in 2005 to support hurricane recovery and long-term economic development in Louisiana, Mississippi, and Alabama. Today, RAND Gulf States provides objective analysis to federal, state, and local leaders in support of evidence-based policymaking and the well-being of individuals throughout the Gulf Coast region. With offices in New Orleans, Louisiana, and Jackson, Mississippi, RAND Gulf States is dedicated to helping the region address a wide range of challenges that include coastal risk reduction and restoration, health care, and workforce development. More information about RAND Gulf States can be found at http://www.rand.org/gulf-states.html.

Contents

Figures

Summary

According to the U.S. Census Bureau, the populations of U.S. coastal counties have grown by more than 45 percent between 1970 and 2010, amounting to 50 million new coastal residents and billions of dollars in additional assets (homes and businesses) in these areas. Coastal residents are vulnerable to many potential risks, including damage to human life and property that results from storm flooding. The increasing concentration of people, property, and other activities in coastal areas can itself contribute to the problem by removing or diminishing wetlands, barrier islands, and other features that serve as natural buffers to storm surges.

The Gulf Coast has borne a substantial portion of the damage from coastal storms in recent decades. For example, in 2005 more than 1,880 people died and thousands more were displaced or left with conditions that compromised their safety, health, and economic well-being due to Hurricane Katrina. Direct damage to New Orleans residences alone is estimated to have reached between $8 billion and $10 billion. But these coastal risks are also prevalent in other areas, as shown by the massive damage and disruption that Hurricane Sandy caused to the people, homes, businesses, and infrastructure of coastal communities along the Eastern Seaboard.

Coastal risks may increase as the climate warms. Sea levels are anywhere from six to 12 inches higher now than a century ago and continue to rise at a rate of more than an inch per decade. Current projections suggest that the rate of sea-level rise will continue to increase because of warming oceans and melting glaciers, leading to sea levels from 8 inches to as much as 4–6 feet higher than 1990 levels by 2100. Such increases, when combined with coastal tides and storm surge, will likely dramatically increase the risk of floods to coastal residents and property. Additionally, warming sea surface temperatures and changing climate patterns could also either intensify future tropical storms and hurricanes or make large and powerful hurricanes more common.

Reducing the vulnerability of coastal communities to these threats is challenging, given both the scale of the problem across broad geographic regions and uncertainty about the specific nature of the risk. Several restoration efforts in the United States have begun to take more-comprehensive planning approaches to addressing such challenges. Those in the Everglades, Chesapeake Bay, and the San Francisco Bay Delta regions are notable recent examples. But such efforts have not yet led to a broadly applicable methodology for identifying and reducing coastal vulnerabilities to climate change.

Although the challenges that coastal Louisiana faces are not unique, the region is a prime example of the need to address coastal planning challenges in a comprehensive way. In Louisiana, storm-surge flood-risk challenges are exacerbated by the loss of land brought on by how the Mississippi River was managed during the past century. Coastal Louisiana is on an unstable path of ongoing land loss. Since the 1930s, nearly 1,900 square miles of land have been lost to open water, and more will be lost in the next 50 years (Couvillion et al., 2011). Spurred on by the devastating effects of hurricanes Katrina and Rita in 2005, the State of Louisiana, through its Coastal Protection and Restoration Authority (CPRA), decided to simultaneously and systematically address both coastal flood risk and ongoing coastal wetland loss by developing Louisiana's Comprehensive Master Plan for a Sustainable Coast.

This Master Plan defines a set of coastal *risk-reduction projects* (both structural projects, including levees, and nonstructural projects that reduce flood damage to residential and commercial structures by, for example, elevating structures) and *restoration projects* (such as bank stabilization, sediment diversions, and barrier island restoration) to be implemented over the next 50 years to reduce hurricane flood risk to coastal communities and to restore the Louisiana coast.

A Framework and Planning Tool to Support Development of the Master Plan

Given the large number of potential projects, the range of stakeholders with competing interests and objectives, and the significant and deep uncertainties to be considered, CPRA asked RAND to support the development of the Master Plan by helping to develop an analytic approach to identify a comprehensive strategy of investments in risk-reduction and restoration projects to address the coast's problems. Part of this mandate was to develop a process that was as objective and transparent as possible and based on the best-available scientific information about coastal processes and flood risk.

Figure S.1 provides a simplified flow chart showing the overall approach. The approach starts by applying a suite of seven interconnected *systems models* to estimate the effects that hundreds of proposed projects could have over the next 50 years on expected flood damage, land building or land loss, and ecosystem services. RAND developed one of these models, the Coastal Louisiana Risk Assessment (CLARA) model, which was used to estimate flood depths and damage that would occur from major storms with and without new risk-reduction investments. The systems models evaluated the effects of each project for two future scenarios that reflect different assumptions about future sea-level rise, the rates at which coastal land subsides (through sediment compaction and other processes), and other key uncertainties about the future: a *moderate* one that assumes low to moderate sea-level rise and subsidence rates, and a *less optimistic* one that assumes much higher values for each. The estimated project effects serve as inputs into the Planning Tool to identify potential alternatives (groups of projects) that could make up the 50-year Master Plan. The Planning Tool uses an optimization model to identify alternatives comprised of risk-reduction projects selected to minimize coast-wide risk to economic assets and restoration projects selected to maximize coast-wide land building, subject to planning constraints related to available future funding, sediment availability, Mississippi River flows, and preferences over a broad range of other outcomes.

The Master Plan Delivery Team[1] used the Planning Tool to formulate hundreds of potential alternatives based on project effects and on the preferences of CPRA senior management and a 33-member stakeholder group consisting of representatives from business and industry; federal, state, and local governments; nongovernmental organizations; and coastal institutions.

---

[1] The Master Plan Delivery Team was comprised of CPRA staff, a consulting team including RAND researchers, university researchers, and representatives from the U.S. Army Corps of Engineers and U.S. Geological Survey.

Figure S.1
Planning Framework Used in Developing the Louisiana 2012 Master Plan

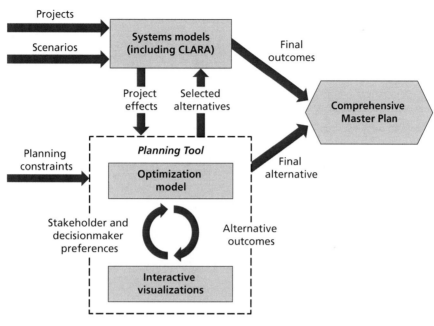

SOURCE: Groves, Fischbach, Knopman, et al., 2013.
RAND *RR437-S.1*

A key part of the Planning Tool, as shown in Figure S.1, is a set of interactive visualizations that present estimates of how alternatives would or would not achieve CPRA's goals. These visualizations allowed CPRA and stakeholders to review and understand the trade-offs among the alternatives during the deliberation process. For example, the Planning Tool enabled stakeholders and decisionmakers to change different input variables—such as the environmental scenario, preferences for ecosystem service outcomes, and specific funding constraints—to understand the effects of these changes on key outputs of interest, such as damage reduction or land building over time.

The Planning Tool was used to identify a final alternative that struck an acceptable balance of investments across different types of projects, coastal regions, near-term and long-term risk reduction and land-building benefits, and projected future ecosystem services. This group of projects was then reevaluated together using the systems models to better understand synergies or trade-offs among the selected projects.

Evaluating Different Risk-Reduction Strategies

Deep uncertainty was a key characteristic of the decisions Louisiana planners faced when developing the Master Plan. In particular, how would the chosen Master Plan perform in terms of risk reduction in either of the two scenarios (with different assumptions about sea-level rise and other uncertainties) 50 years in the future?

As shown in Figure S.1, a suite of systems models was used to evaluate the effects of different projects on the coast over different scenarios reflecting uncertainty. One of those was the CLARA model, used to estimate flood depths and damage that occur as a result of major storms. CLARA made it possible to systematically evaluate potential projects for the Master Plan based on how well they reduce storm-surge flood damage in Louisiana's coastal region. The results from CLARA show that, without the Master Plan's protection and restoration projects, storm-surge flood damage represents a major threat to coastal Louisiana. All told, CLARA includes a level of detail suitable for rigorously performing comparative evaluations of many options while accounting for a wide range of future uncertainties, including those emerging from a changing climate. Beyond its help in developing the current Master Plan, CLARA can also serve as a road map for future evaluations of coastal flood damage or damage reduction in Louisiana and other coastal regions.

Flood-damage results developed with CLARA show that storm-surge flood damage represents a major threat to coastal Louisiana and that, if no action is taken, this damage can be expected to grow significantly in the future (Figure S.2). The increase in flood damage, however, varies substantially across the two scenarios considered in the 2012 Master Plan. These scenarios differed across many uncertain factors, including sea-level rise, subsidence, and storm frequency and intensity. For instance, in 2061, expected annual damage (EAD) is projected to increase to between $7 billion and $21 billion without action, depending on whether the scenario included moderate, middle-of-the-road assumptions or whether the scenario included less optimistic assumptions (purple bars). But, with the Master Plan in place, this damage level is reduced to between $3 billion and $5 billion for the two scenarios (beige bars). This corresponds to a reduction of approximately 60 percent to almost 80 percent compared with flood-damage levels in the future without action.

Figure S.3 shows CLARA results coast-wide for how the portfolio of projects included in the Master Plan can help to reduce flood damage. The projects associated with the Master

Figure S.2
Reduction in Coast-Wide EAD With and Without the Master Plan

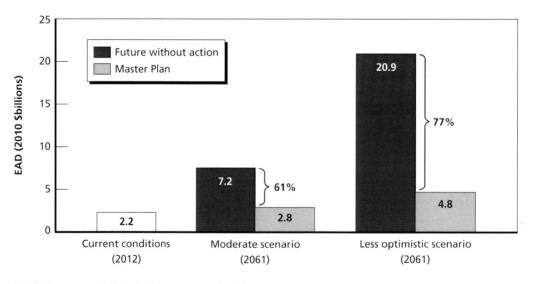

SOURCE: Groves, Fischbach, Knopman, et al., 2013.
NOTE: EAD represents the average damage projected to occur from a storm surge flooding event from a Category 3 or greater storm in any given year, taking into account both the projected damage and the overall chance of such a storm occurring.
RAND *RR437-S.2*

Figure S.3
Reduction in 100-Year Flood Depths in 50 Years Due to the Master Plan (Less Optimistic Scenario)

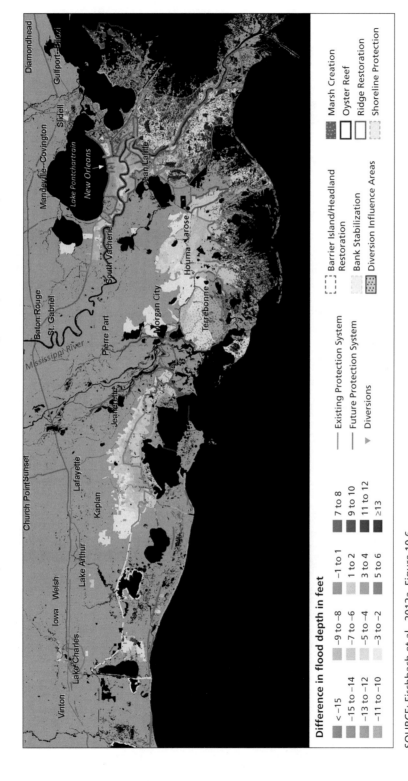

SOURCE: Fischbach et al., 2012a, Figure 10.6.
NOTE: The 100-year flood is the flood depth that has a 1-percent chance of occurring in any year.
RAND RR437-S.3

Plan are indicated on the map, and include structural protection (in pink), river diversions to rebuild wetlands, and other coastal restoration projects. Areas marked in blue on the map face deeper levels of flooding; areas marked in orange face less flooding.

Using a Planning Tool to Compare Protection and Restoration Projects and Develop a Comprehensive Plan

One of the key benefits of Louisiana's Master Plan approach is the use of objective, scientific information, such as the results generated from the systems models (e.g., CLARA), within a quantitative framework that enables the development and comparison of different strategies and supports deliberations among them. Interactive visualizations are useful to ensure that decisionmakers understand the key trade-offs among strategies.

For example, because land building is an important goal, the Planning Tool identified a series of sediment diversion, marsh creation, and other restoration projects that are likely to lead to the most land building over the 50-year planning horizon. This alternative includes several large sediment-diversion projects. But policymakers face other decision criteria beyond maximizing land building. One key criterion is preserving habitat for different species of aquatic life in the Gulf, and large sediment diversions can affect that habitat. This is because such projects, which are very effective at building land in the long term, also decrease the salinity of shallow wetlands where many aquatic species spend a portion of their lives.

This trade-off is reflected in Figure S.4, which shows changes in land in square miles from 2012 to 2061, along with the likely effects on habitats of saltwater aquatic species. The "without action" alternative results in the significant loss of about 700 square miles and shows a slight increase in the saltwater species' habitat. Conversely, the "maximize land building" alternative leads to stabilization of coast-wide land area over time but would lead to a significant decline in

Figure S.4
Trade-Offs Between Land Building and Area of Suitable Saltwater Habitat

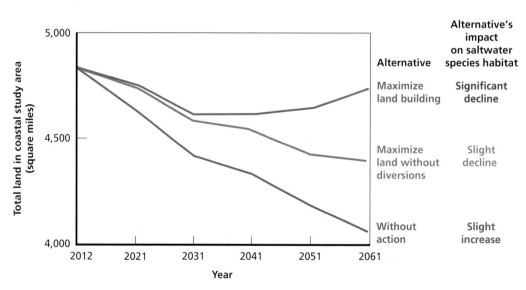

SOURCE: Groves, Fischbach, Knopman, et al., 2013.
RAND RR437-S.4

the saltwater species' habitat. The Planning Tool also created another alternative: "maximize land without diversions." Although this alternative leads to only a slight decline in the saltwater species' habitat, it would not achieve the state's objective of stabilizing the coast-wide land area. This trade-off analysis led the state to consider additional alternatives (not shown here) in which sediment diversions were used (sparingly) to strike the right balance between land building and support for all aquatic habitats.

The Planning Tool does not tell policymakers *which* alternative to choose. Rather, it allows them to visualize what the trade-offs are in choosing one alternative over another. In deciding on the Master Plan, policymakers actually needed to understand the implications of trying to balance multiple decision criteria (not just saltwater species' habitat) relative to the ultimate goal of the sustainability of the landscape.

How Louisiana's Experience Can Inform Coastal Resilience Planning Elsewhere

This work provides a successful example of how integrated, objective, analysis-based planning can address pressing coastal challenges. By using this analytic approach, CPRA was able to develop a $50 billion, 50-year Master Plan. The planning processes helped CPRA and stakeholders grapple with tough trade-offs between "hard" (infrastructure) and "soft" (restoration and nonstructural mitigation) approaches to coastal resilience and sustainability. Concurrently, it helped CPRA consider how different future scenarios would affect the success of different approaches.

The resulting Master Plan is the first comprehensive solution for Louisiana's coast to receive broad support from the Louisiana public and the many agencies—federal, state, and local—engaged in protecting the Gulf Coast. It passed the Louisiana legislature unanimously in May 2012 and is currently being implemented. And, with the analytic infrastructure in place, this approach will also help as CPRA takes steps to secure long-term funding, refine its near-term implementation strategy, and adapt the Master Plan over time as assumptions change.

Coastal Louisiana is only one of many areas of the nation dealing with such challenges. In just the last decade, coastal storms such as hurricanes Ivan (2004), Charley (2004), Katrina (2005), Rita (2005), Gustav (2008), Ike (2008), Isaac (2012), and Sandy (2012) have changed lives and economies along U.S. coastlines.

The Mid-Atlantic States—following Hurricane Sandy—and other coastal regions are facing challenges in planning similar to those faced by Louisiana. In each of these regions

- coastal risks are increasing, but in uncertain ways
- there are many different types of strategies to consider to reduce risks and restore coastal landscapes
- solutions will be implemented by local, regional, state, and federal agencies.

Given the uncertainty of how these factors—alone or in combination—will play out in a given region, coastal regions and communities are in need of a new approach to developing coastal resilience plans with actionable strategies. Our work in Louisiana and elsewhere suggests that the approach should be based on three principles:

- Public participation is essential throughout the planning process to understand the preferences and local knowledge relevant to the decisions and to ensure credibility and legitimacy of the technical analysis.
- Technical analysis is meant to inform deliberations and value judgments by decisionmakers rather than provide a single answer that is then "sold" to affected constituencies.
- A successful and sustainable long-term strategy must be robust and adaptive—one which includes near-term investments that are shown to provide a strong foundation for future decisions that would be made in response to conditions that are revealed over time.

The application of this approach and these principles can help that region assimilate different goals or points of view and disparate and potentially conflicting technical analyses into a framework to identify a robust strategy for recovery and future risk reduction. Other coastal areas could also benefit from the application of this approach, including the Eastern Seaboard, as it seeks to be better prepared for sea-level rise and future storms, and California, as it seeks to address its vulnerability to sea-level rise and other threats to its Sacramento–San Joaquin River Delta.

Acknowledgments

We would like to thank the staff of the Coastal Protection and Restoration Authority of Louisiana for their support of our work throughout the development of the Master Plan. We would especially like to thank CPRA's Natalie Peyronnin, Karim Belhadjali, Mandy Green, Melanie Saucier, and Carol Parsons Richards; Kirk Rhinehart, formerly with CPRA; Denise Reed, now with the Water Institute of the Gulf; and our many other collaborators, in particular those at Brown and Caldwell and Arcadis.

This report received generous funding from a fund established to support and promote policy innovation at RAND. We are grateful for this institutional support. We appreciate the assistance of David Manheim of the Pardee RAND Graduate School with background research, RAND's Paul Steinberg for his input to the summary, and RAND's Paul Davis for his thorough and thoughtful peer review. Finally, we would like to thank Keith Crane, Director of the Environment, Energy, and Economic Development Program, for his assistance throughout the effort and Anna Smith for helping see the document through to completion.

Abbreviations

AEP	annual exceedance probability
CLARA	Coastal Louisiana Risk Assessment
CPRA	(Louisiana) Coastal Protection and Restoration Authority
EAD	expected annual damage
FEMA	Federal Emergency Management Agency
RDM	Robust Decision Making

CHAPTER ONE

Introduction

In August 2005, Hurricane Katrina's landfall in Louisiana reminded the nation of coastal communities' vulnerability to storm surges and flooding (Figure 1.1). More than 1,880 people died and thousands more were displaced or left with conditions that compromised their safety, health, and economic well-being. Direct damage to New Orleans residences alone is estimated to have reached between $8 billion and $10 billion (Brinkley, 2006; Grossi and Muir-Wood, 2006). While the region was home to one of the most extensive hurricane protection systems in the world, it was clear once again that flood risks were unacceptably high and that the accelerating loss of land since the 1930s, if continued unabated, would exacerbate these risks and threaten the viability of coastal Louisiana's communities and economy.

Louisiana, like many coastal regions, has struggled for decades to develop a sustainable and effective plan to address the range of natural and manmade forces that have led to continu-

Figure 1.1
Flood Damage After Hurricane Katrina, 2005

SOURCE: U.S. Army photo by SSC Ricky R. Melton.
RAND *RR437-1.1*

ing loss of coastal lands. Over the years, various interests in the region had advanced a diverse range and large number of possible solutions, but never had the state had a means of evaluating them on the same analytical terms, separately or together. Scientists and engineers over time had developed a number of options for restoring coastal features and reducing flood risk, but the state lacked clarity as to which to implement and how to integrate them. Further, Louisiana, like all coastal regions, faces deep uncertainty about future conditions and the effects of actions. The pace and degree of global climate change is as of yet unknown, and how projects might perform over the long term or what wider effects they could have on the coastal environment is uncertain. Current projections, for example, suggest that sea levels will continue to rise to between 8 inches and 4–6 feet over 1990 levels by 2100 because of warming oceans and melting glaciers (Parris et al., 2012). Warming sea surface temperatures and changing climate patterns could also either intensify future tropical storms and hurricanes or make large and powerful hurricanes more common (Intergovernmental Panel on Climate Change, 2012; Intergovernmental Panel on Climate Change, 2013). Policymakers in Louisiana and other coastal regions need a means of addressing complexities and uncertainties in planning to raise the odds of success despite likely changes and surprises in the future.

Louisiana also has had to grapple with diverse and conflicting goals and objectives that have hindered creation of a single comprehensive plan in the past. Lack of consensus about goals and priorities can hinder any region's best planning efforts, and in the past this had certainly been the case in Louisiana. Finally, coastal regions have a need for coordination across jurisdictions, as activities to improve flood protection and improve the coastal system involve many local communities, local and regional levee boards, state and federal agencies, and private-sector interests. Furthermore, given limited available funding, coordinated planning is essential to support a process to make the necessary trade-offs in how resources are spent across the coast.

This report synthesizes RAND's work with Louisiana's Coastal Protection and Restoration Authority (CPRA) in its development of the *2012 Comprehensive Master Plan for a Sustainable Coast*, with the goal of helping policymakers in other coastal regions develop and evaluate strategies to reduce flood risk, rebuild or restore coastal environments, and more generally increase the resilience of developed coastlines. It is intended to serve as a guide to foster new conversations among policymakers, stakeholders, and residents concerned with the well-being of coastal regions in the United States and elsewhere in the world.

Forces at Work on the Louisiana Coast

Louisiana's coastline has always been dynamic—expanding and receding over the course of millennia in response to periodic flooding and sediment deposition from the Mississippi and Atchafalaya rivers and their distributaries, wave and wind actions from the sea, and gradual settling and sinking (land subsidence). As the coastline developed and the U.S. Army Corps of Engineers channelized the Mississippi River to improve navigation and river flood control, the natural sedimentation process has been disrupted and sea-level rise and subsidence have combined to reduce coastal land and increase vulnerability of the Louisiana coast to storm damage.

A Modified River Runs Through It

Louisiana's coastal plain was formed from the deposit of nourishing sediment from the Mississippi River in a series of deltaic cycles thousands of years ago. These natural cycles have been interrupted in recent times by decades of infrastructure building and altered land use practices as coastal development accelerated. Flood-control measures—primarily levees along the major rivers built over the last century—have all but eliminated the natural river flood re-sedimentation of much of the state's coastal wetlands. Today, the Mississippi River primarily deposits sediments deep into the Gulf of Mexico rather than along the coast, leading to rapid coastal land loss in response to natural geologic subsidence and ocean dynamics. Sea-level rise is accelerating this land loss, as are natural oil and gas extraction and other industrial activities that contribute to coastal erosion and subsidence (Dokka, 2006; Penland and Ramsey, 1990; U.S. Army Corps of Engineers, 2011). Other commercial and navigational activities have also taken a toll. For example, over 9,000 miles of navigation canals have been cut into Louisiana wetlands in recent decades (Reed and Wilson, 2004). These changes have negatively impacted the rich coastal ecosystem, while also degrading natural coastal defenses to storm surge flooding. This, in turn, puts Louisiana's communities at increasing risk of disaster.

Business as Usual Will Not Halt the Land Loss

Since the 1930s, nearly 1,900 square miles of land—mostly wetlands—have converted to open water in southern Louisiana (Couvillion et al., 2011). The loss of this land, comparable in area to the state of Rhode Island, has profoundly changed the nature of the coastal environment. At the current rate of land loss, between 800 and 1,750 square miles of land are at risk of disappearing over the next 50 years (Coastal Protection and Restoration Authority of Louisiana, 2012a). The less optimistic estimate of possible coastal land loss over the next 50 years without significant restoration is depicted in Figure 1.2. Notice that under these projections, much of the remaining wetlands between coastal communities, such as New Orleans, and the ocean would be gone and entire swaths of the central and western portion of the state would be lost.

The Risk of Coastal Flooding Is Rising

Wetlands, barrier islands, dunes, ridges, and other natural coastal features historically have played a very important role as Louisiana's first line of defense against storm surge and waves caused by hurricanes and tropical storms. As these features have eroded, leaving open water in their place, the waves and surge associated with hurricanes and tropical storms can penetrate unimpeded much closer to Louisiana's vital infrastructure. As Figure 1.3 illustrates, the depth of flooding from a 100-year event, or one with a 1-percent chance of occurring in any year, will increase all across the coast—in some cases by more than 10 feet. Some of the largest increases in flood depth would be experienced in the Greater New Orleans region, the Larose to Golden Meadow protection system (south of New Orleans), and in the expanding communities on the north shore of Lake Pontchartrain. Expected annual damage (EAD)[1] from all major hurricane flooding events (Category 3 hurricanes or higher) could increase to between $7 billion and $21 billion in a future without action.

---

[1]   EAD represents the average damage projected to occur from a storm surge flooding event from a Category 3 or greater storm in any given year, taking into account both the projected damage and the overall chance of such a storm occurring.

Figure 1.2
Significant Coastal Land Loss over the Next 50 Years Without a Plan

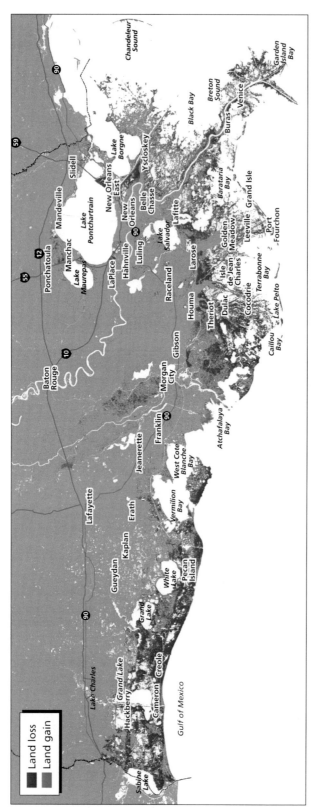

SOURCE: CPRA, 2012a.

RAND RR437-1.2

Figure 1.3
Increase in 100-Year Flood Depths from 2012 to 2061 in One Plausible Scenario

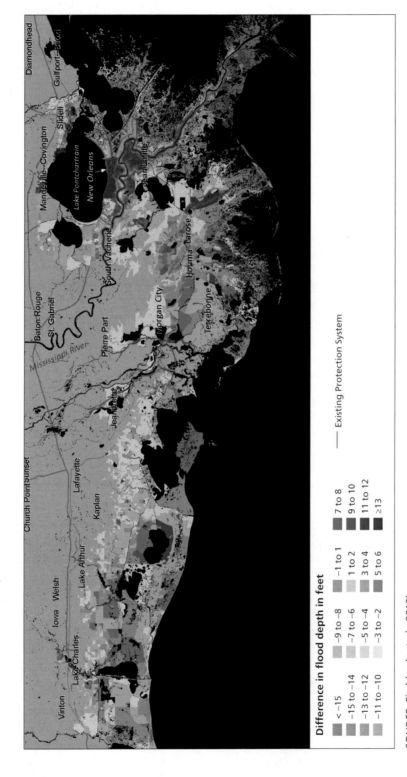

Difference in flood depth in feet

<–15	–9 to –8	–1 to 1	7 to 8
–15 to –14	–7 to –6	1 to 2	9 to 10
–13 to –12	–5 to –4	3 to 4	11 to 12
–11 to –10	–3 to –2	5 to 6	≥13

—— Existing Protection System

SOURCE: Fischbach et al., 2012b.
Note: This estimate is for the "Less Optimistic" scenario developed for Louisiana's 2012 Master Plan.

RAND RR437-1.3

Economic and Social Implications of a Coast at Risk

The loss of coastal wetlands and increasing vulnerability of coastal communities threatens the economic and social status quo of the region and the nation. Louisiana's Master Plan enumerates the assets and services the coast provides and, ultimately, what is at stake if no changes were to be made (Coastal Protection and Restoration Authority of Louisiana, 2012a):

- **90 percent of the nation's outer continental oil and gas supply:** Louisiana is one of the nation's primary energy hubs, and the energy production and distribution infrastructure could be severely compromised by land loss. Coastal land loss increases the vulnerability of the extensive infrastructure.
- **20 percent of the nation's annual waterborne commerce:** Southern Louisiana is critical to national and international trade. Ten major navigation routes run through five major ports in the region, handling approximately 20 percent of annual U.S. waterborne commerce. Coastal land loss increases the vulnerability of the ports.
- **26 percent (by weight) of continental U.S. commercial fisheries:** Fish, as well as shrimp, oysters, and blue crabs, thrive in the region. Continued rapid changes to the landscape threaten the viability of many commercial fisheries in the region.
- **5 million birds' winter homes:** Louisiana's coastal wetlands provide a winter habitat for migratory birds and nesting habitats for local waterfowl. Continued rapid changes to the landscape threaten the diversity of habitat and lifecycles of birds and other wildlife.

Also at stake is a way of life. Hundreds of thousands of coastal residents depend on these resources for employment, and over two million call the region their home.

Challenges in Creating a Master Plan

For more than three decades, national and state government agencies, state and local organizations, corporations, and citizen's groups have been aware of Louisiana's degrading coast and have invested significant resources in restoring damages and stopping further deterioration in selected areas. These efforts, however, were clearly not sufficient to halt coastal land loss and the accompanying ecosystem degradation, or to reduce flood risks to acceptable levels. The 2005 hurricanes made clear that more action was required and that to be effective it would need to be coordinated as part of a comprehensive plan.

A number of challenges impeded the creation of a single, actionable plan prior to the 2012 Master Plan.

Diverse Range and Large Number of Possible Solutions

Over the years, scientists, engineers, and local planners in Louisiana had developed a host of projects designed to shore up vulnerable eroding coastlines, rebuild wetlands that have converted to open water, block storm surges to reduce flooding, and in some cases restore natural riverine and sedimentation processes in different areas of the coast. Specifically, restoration projects have been designed for bank stabilization, barrier island restoration, channel realignment, marsh creation through river and sediment diversions, marsh creation though mechanical means, restoration of natural hydrologic conditions, oyster barrier reef, ridge restoration, and shoreline protection. Risk-reduction projects have included both "structural" and "non-structural" projects. Structural projects, such as levees and floodwalls, are designed to block or reroute water, altering the geographic distribution of flooding. "Nonstructural" projects are those that reduce the vulnerability to flooding of individual assets, such as residential and commercial structures, by elevating, floodproofing, or buying out and removing structures from the floodplain (Figure 1.4). Yet the cost and performance of each project varies widely, and the projects may work toward some of the region's goals while working against some others.

The Future Is Uncertain

Future coastal conditions and threats in Louisiana are highly uncertain. Rates of sea-level rise, land subsidence and erosion rates, future hurricane activity, hydrologic fluctuations and trends, ecosystem and species' responses, and development and industrial activities, are all but impossible to predict in the long run, despite our best scientific understanding of these processes. This uncertainty complicates the development of a strategy for the Louisiana coastline. A strategy that would be expected to perform well for some future conditions may perform significantly less well in others. Thus, the traditional planning approach of predicting the future and then developing a strategy for that prediction would not suffice.

CPRA was in need of a plan that could succeed in the presence of continuing complexities, uncertainties, anticipated changes, and surprises. To ensure success under the actual

Figure 1.4
Wide Diversity in Options for Addressing Land Loss and Flood Risk

SOURCES: Clockwise from top left: CPRA, 2012a, pp. 41–42; CPRA, 2012a, p. 69; CPRA, 2012a, pp. 164–165; CPRA, 2012a, p. 70.
RAND *RR437-1.4*

future conditions that might prevail, the state sought a robust and adaptive strategy. Such a strategy for Louisiana would (1) identify near-term investments that would be sensible over a wide range of plausible future conditions, (2) identify coastal conditions that should be monitored to serve as signposts for future modifications in the plan, and (3) lay out different alternatives for future investments that would need to be made depending on how the future unfolds.

A Diverse Region Seeking Different and Sometimes Conflicting Outcomes

The Louisiana coast is endowed with a large diversity of natural resources, many of which support economic and recreational activities. The coast is also home to large cities, such as New Orleans, with significant existing flood control infrastructure constructed by the federal government, and smaller communities, such as Houma, that have little or none; what protection does exist is often constructed and maintained only by local levee boards. Any decision that affects a community and the environment is subject to debate over goals and priorities, jurisdiction, and resource allocation. Trade-offs among objectives often lead to winners and losers. The Master Plan needed to reflect the preferences of the state's leadership as well as account for the views within the 33-member stakeholder group consisting of representatives from business and industry; federal, state, and local governments; nongovernmental organizations; and other coastal institutions.

Need for Coordination Across Jurisdictions

Storm-surge flooding does not stop at political boundaries, and the implications of wetland loss can extend far beyond the immediate coastal area. While Louisiana's coastal planning challenges are regional, with national implications, they are affected by local, regional, state, and federal actions. If each locality is working only in its own best interest, solutions are less likely to address the larger set of issues most salient at the regional level. Further, local resources are often too constrained to address their own concerns adequately, much less to consider the larger impact that their actions have on neighboring areas.

In Louisiana, many small-scale or localized restoration projects have been constructed along the coast in recent decades. The net gain from these projects, however, has been small compared to the substantial land loss occurring coast-wide. Furthermore, lack of coordination between hurricane protection and restoration efforts has likely led to worse outcomes for both objectives: Levees can hasten coastal wetland degradation, which in turn degrades the natural barrier these wetlands can provide against storm surge (Coastal Protection and Restoration Authority of Louisiana, 2007; Lopez et al., 2009).

Evolution of the Master Planning Process

Following the devastating 2005 hurricane season, Louisiana took the first steps in the release of its 2007 Comprehensive Master Plan (Coastal Protection and Restoration Authority of Louisiana, 2007). The 2007 Master Plan set a new course for Louisiana by defining four high-level objectives to guide development of a comprehensive strategy:

- reduce risk to economic assets
- restore sustainability to the coastal ecosystem
- maintain a diverse array of habitats for fish and wildlife

- sustain Louisiana's unique heritage and culture.

These objectives were intended to guide the state's long-term infrastructure investments on the coast. Underlying this approach was the idea of *multiple lines of defense*: combining restoration of the natural environment, engineered infrastructure, more resilient building practices, and improved emergency management and evacuation planning, all to ensure that overall risk from flooding to people and property on the coast is minimized (Lopez et al., 2009). The 2007 Master Plan did not, however, provide a quantified comparison of costs and benefits for the many proposed projects, consider a wide variety of future scenarios, or define a preferred set of projects to meet these long-term goals. This plan was then significantly enhanced for 2012 (Coastal Protection and Restoration Authority of Louisiana, 2012a).

RAND researchers supported the 2012 Master Planning effort by first helping to develop a decisionmaking framework to understand which short-term and large-scale efforts would be needed to restore, protect, and sustain Louisiana's coastal communities and landscape, and then by developing two specific modeling tools. In the next chapter, we describe the framework and models developed to support this effort.

CHAPTER TWO

Analytical Support for the Development of Louisiana's 50-Year Comprehensive Plan

In this chapter, we describe two key analytic capabilities developed to support the Master Plan process: the systems models,[1] including the Coastal Louisiana Risk Assessment Model (CLARA), and the Planning Tool.[2] In the following chapter, we describe the kinds of assessments and decisionmaking the Planning Tool enhanced, and which ultimately supported CPRA in defining a plan to achieving its coastal protection and restoration goals.

New Analytical Capabilities Informed the Planning Framework

The analytic framework consists of a combination of two sets of analytic capabilities: systems modeling (including CLARA) and the CPRA Planning Tool. Figure 2.1 illustrates the framework in flowchart form and is described in detail in the subsequent subsections.

The beginning of the process is represented at the top left of the flow chart. Analysis began by evaluating how hundreds of proposed coastal restoration and protection projects would affect the coast over the next 50 years relative to no action for multiple future scenarios, using a suite of seven systems models. CLARA was one of these models. Together, the systems models evaluated the effects that each project would have on the coastal landscape, including barrier islands and wetlands; on future storm surges, waves, flooding, and flood damage; and on ecosystem characteristics, including habitats for different aquatic and land-based species. Additional calculations provided rough assessments of impacts on navigation, cultural heritage, the oil and gas industry, and other key assets.

The models' results served as inputs to the Planning Tool, a computer-based decision support software system, along with planning constraints such as availability of sediment and river flow, available funding over the next five decades, and the preferences of CPRA senior management and the group of stakeholders. The Planning Tool uses optimization to iteratively identify alternatives comprised of the most cost-effective projects that build land and reduce flood risk while meeting different planning constraints and stakeholder preferences. The Planning Tool

---

[1] The Master Plan and other derivative works refer to the systems models as "predictive models." We describe them in this report as "systems models" to focus on their use as tools to integrate our current level of understanding of the coastal system rather than "predict" the future. These mathematical models will continue to be refined over time as new data and understanding of physical processes increases.

[2] Full documentation of these tools is provided in Johnson, Fischbach, and Ortiz, 2013; Fischbach et al., 2012a; Groves and Sharon, 2013; and Groves, Sharon, and Knopman, 2012.

Figure 2.1
Framework Developed to Support the Master Plan

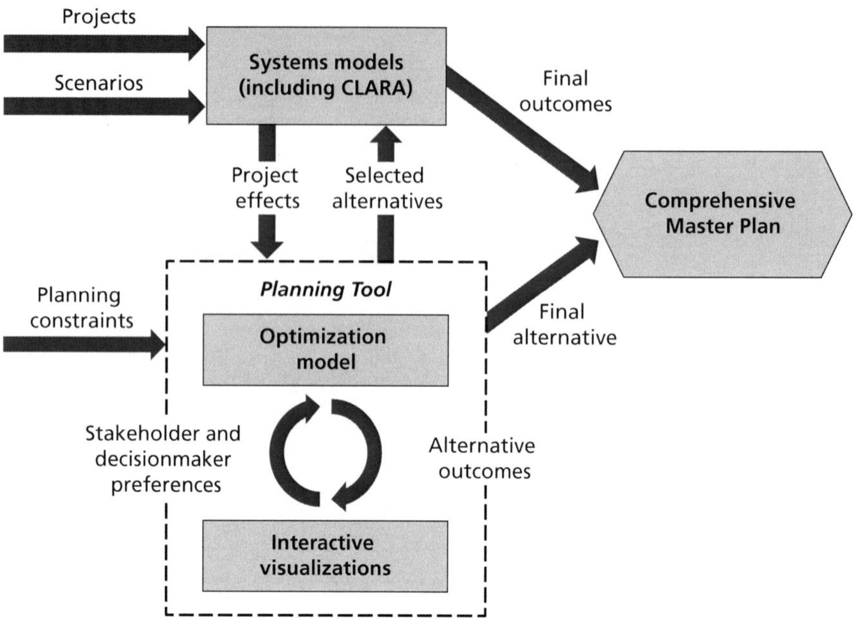

SOURCE: Groves, Fischbach, Knopman, et al., 2013.
RAND *RR437-2.1*

generates interactive visualizations that summarize information about trade-offs among individual projects and alternatives.

The Planning Tool was first used to help assess the overall benefits and costs of hundreds of proposed protection and restoration projects. CPRA next used the Planning Tool as part of an iterative participatory decision process to develop a large set of different alternatives—groups of individual projects—and then identify a small set of alternatives that were considered as the foundation of the final Master Plan. These selected alternatives were then run through the systems models again and reevaluated to better understand synergies or trade-offs among the included projects.

Accounting for Deep Uncertainty Using Scenarios

Both the Planning Tool and CLARA were designed to account for the substantial uncertainty that complicates planning for coastal restoration and protection. How well any set of structural protection or coastal restoration projects reduces flood risk depends substantially on many uncertain factors. For example, how fast future sea level rises can determine which marsh building projects would be most desirable to implement. The severity of future coastal storms can significantly affect flood risk under different proposed levee alignments.

CPRA strived to develop a Master Plan that is robust to as much uncertainty about these future conditions as possible, given time and resource constraints for developing the Master Plan. Thus, the modeling teams developed three environmental scenarios to help identify near-term investments that could perform sufficiently well over a range of future conditions and determine which other investments could be implemented successfully at later points in time.

The first two environmental scenarios were referred to as *moderate* and *less optimistic*. The moderate scenario was designed to reflect generally middle-of-the-road assumptions about future conditions. The less optimistic scenario was designed to represent conditions that would lead to less desirable outcomes for Louisiana—specifically less land and higher flood risk. A third environmental scenario, *moderate with high sea-level rise*, was developed toward the end of the process to better understand the effects of sea-level rise that was higher than that in the less optimistic scenario, but was not highlighted in the Master Plan.

These do not represent "best-" or "worst-case" futures. Instead, they represent possible future conditions built from the value ranges of specific uncertainties. Environmental uncertainties considered included sea-level rise, land subsidence, hurricane frequency, hurricane intensity, Mississippi River discharge, rainfall, evapotranspiration, Mississippi River nutrient concentration, and a parameter that is used to estimate when marsh growth can no longer offset sea-level rise and subsidence. Socioeconomic and operational uncertainties also were considered. These included coastal population growth; the relative concentration of urban and rural populations; the effectiveness of pumping systems; the likelihood that levees and other structural facilities will fail under stress; and the effectiveness of nonstructural programs designed to reduce risks through floodproofing, elevating homes, or relocations. The modeling teams used pertinent scientific literature and expert judgment to determine how to represent these uncertain factors in the environmental scenarios. The details of the scenarios are described in full in Appendix C of the Master Plan (Coastal Protection and Restoration Authority of Louisiana, 2012b).

CPRA also developed scenarios for annual funding over the next 50 years by evaluating a wide variety of funding sources and estimating a range of potential funds from each source over time. From these ranges, two primary scenarios were defined: a low-funding scenario (totaling about $20 billion over 50 years) and a high-funding scenario (totaling about $50 billion over 50 years). CPRA also developed additional scenarios, including a $100 billion funding scenario in which CPRA would have $2 billion per year to spend on implementing the Master Plan (Groves, Sharon, and Knopman, 2012).

While the evaluation of these uncertain factors through three future scenarios is an important first step toward developing a robust coastal strategy, more systematic stress testing of the Master Plan is required. Given time and other constraints, the modeling conducted for the 2012 Master Plan could support neither a systematic determination of which environmental factors were most critical nor which specific ranges of these factors could lead the Master Plan to fail to achieve its goals. As one example, the analysis does not provide information on how much the sea level could rise before it would undermine the estimated performance of the Master Plan.

The environmental scenarios used to illustrate the performance of the Master Plan were also developed prior to the evaluation of the selected Master Plan. There may be other plausible scenarios not evaluated that would suggest that elements of the Master Plan are less robust than they seem based on analysis to date. Fortunately, the framework developed for the Master Plan is intended to be adapted to changing conditions and improved understanding, and to accommodate a more extensive robustness analysis that could be conducted as part of the 2017 Master Plan update.

Systems Models, CLARA, and Innovative Flood Risk Modeling

The systems models (including CLARA, discussed below) were used to estimate the effects of risk-reduction projects on expected flood damage across 56 communities in coastal Louisiana. They also estimated the effects of restoration projects on 14 ecosystem-service metrics across 12 coastal regions (Groves, Sharon, and Knopman, 2012).

CLARA was used to evaluate potential damage from coastal flooding, represented as direct damage to physical property on the Louisiana coast. Of course, coastal flooding can bring other risks important for planning, such as the potential for large-scale loss of life or a major shock to the regional or national economy. Louisiana policymakers chose to use direct damage at different levels of severity as a proxy for this broader range of risks when developing the Master Plan, under the basic assumption that flood events that produce widespread property damage would also be much more likely to produce these other bad outcomes.

CLARA is based on the principles of quantitative risk analysis (Fischbach et al., 2012a; Johnson, Fischbach, and Ortiz, 2013). Risk is typically described as the product of the probability or likelihood of a given event occurring and the event's consequences. CLARA aggregates the flood and damage results from a wide range of potential storm events to calculate the chance that any given level of flooding or damage would occur. CLARA uses this information to generate annual exceedance probabilities (AEPs), which refer to flood depth or damage levels that have a specified probability of occurring or being exceeded in a given year.

To consider flood damage at different levels of severity and likelihood, CLARA estimates 2 percent, 1 percent, and 0.2 percent AEP values for flood depths at each point across coastal Louisiana; these are commonly referred to as 50-, 100-, and 500-year flood depths, respectively. The model also estimates 50-, 100-, and 500-year damage values in each census block, based on the corresponding flood depth exceedances, the types and values of assets within that block, and the time required to reconstruct or repair the ensuing property damage.

CLARA also produced estimates of expected annual damage (EAD), which can be thought of as the average damage from storm-surge–based flooding in a given year if one were to smooth out damage across years in a uniform way. EAD takes into account the uncertain timing of severe floods; Regions may be severely flooded in a year or several years, or may experience no flooding or minor flooding over years or decades, and this metric provides a convenient way to average these numbers over time. The typical frequency of storms is combined with the distribution of damage contingent on a storm occurring to estimate the damaged expected in any single year.

The RAND risk-and-damage team developed CLARA to systematically evaluate hundreds of risk-reduction projects for possible inclusion in the Master Plan on the basis of how well they reduce flood damage in Louisiana's coastal region (Fischbach et al., 2012a; Johnson, Fischbach, and Ortiz, 2013). The model was intended to provide a high-level, initial assessment of risk in many plausible futures, looking ahead 50 years, rather than a more detailed snapshot of risk in a single scenario only. As such, the team made a series of simplifying assumptions to balance the level of detail included with the computational and time constraints faced during Master Plan development. Many portions of the model were drawn from and compared to existing, previously vetted efforts conducted by the Federal Emergency Management Agency (FEMA) (2013) and the U.S. Army Corps of Engineers (2009), and the modeled representations of physical processes, such as storm surge and waves, were extensively validated against recent storm events by our partner team, Arcadis (Cobell et al., 2013). However, the CLARA model itself was not validated with historical flood events for the Master Plan analysis.

The structure of the CLARA model is illustrated in Figure 2.2. In the input preprocessing module, CLARA uses information about the study region and generates flood depth estimates in areas outside of enclosed hurricane protection systems, as well as the storm hazard conditions for a collection of hypothetical storms. It also records surge and wave conditions along the external boundaries of protection structures.

In the flood depth module, CLARA focuses on flooding within enclosed protection systems, such as in New Orleans. For these areas, this module is used to estimate "overtopping," that is, the volume of water that could flow over structures into protected areas. The module also considers the possibility that levees or other protection structures might fail. CLARA handles this "system fragility" using a simplified approach that brackets between two extreme cases: one in which protection systems never fail, and one in which breaches result in a flood height inside the levee system that equals the peak storm surge height outside of the breach.

In the economic module, CLARA values the assets at risk from flooding and estimates damage. Damage is estimated by census block at the 50-, 100-, and 500-year damage exceedances. Damage depends on the inventory of assets, so we built an inventory of assets (e.g., homes, roads, and agricultural buildings and crops) within each census block and placed a value on the assets and their contents. Values depend on characteristics that vary by asset type. For example, single-family homes are valued at replacement cost per square foot, which in turn depends on a number of factors related to their construction. The CLARA model largely bases its inventory and value assumptions on FEMA's Hazards United States Multi-Hazard (Hazus-MH) model, 2010 census data, and Louisiana-specific data provided by the Louisiana Coastal Protection and Restoration project. In addition to property damage, CLARA estimates the costs borne by victims who are displaced by flooding (Coastal Protection and Restoration Authority of Louisiana, 2007; Fischbach et al., 2012a; Johnson, Fischbach, and Ortiz, 2013; Federal Emergency Management Agency, 2013).

With CLARA, CPRA analyzed three time periods and three scenarios: 2012 (conditions current at the time the study began), 2036 (25 years from present), and 2061 (50 years from present), in the moderate, moderate with high sea-level rise, and less optimistic future sce-

Figure 2.2
Structure of the CLARA Model

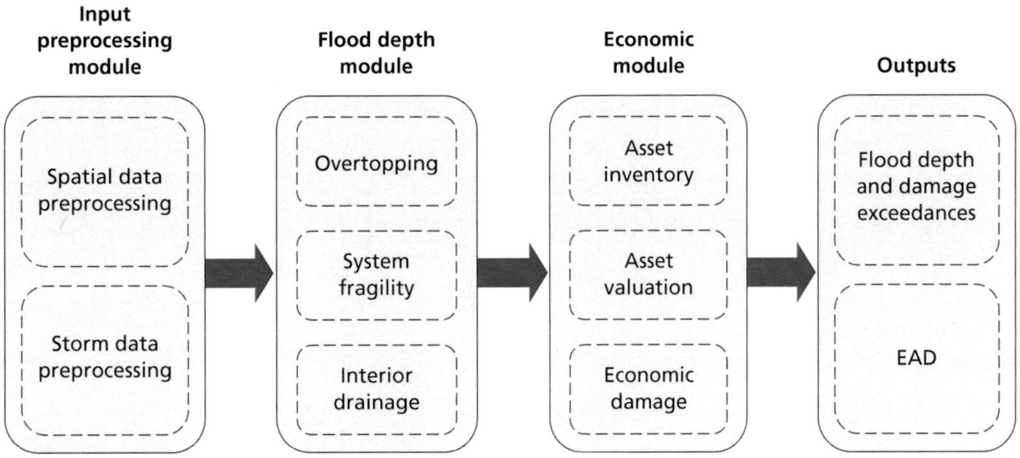

SOURCE: Fischbach et al., 2012a, Figure S.1.
RAND *RR437-2.2*

narios. Most relevant to flood risk, these scenarios reflect different assumptions regarding sea-level rise, the rates by which coastal land subsides, and future hurricane characteristics. The moderate scenario assumes low to moderate sea-level rise and subsidence rates, while the less optimistic scenario uses much less conservative assumptions.

Figure 1.3 in the preceding chapter illustrates the potential increase in flood depths over 50 years in a future without action. Figure 3.5 in the next chapter shows, through CLARA modeling, how the portfolio of projects included in the Master Plan can help to reduce flood depths in the same areas.

The Planning Tool and Innovative Decisionmaking

CPRA asked RAND to develop a Planning Tool to help use the information from the systems models, including CLARA, to support the formulation of the Master Plan. As shown in the flowchart in Figure 2.1, the Planning Tool assimilates information on how projects would affect storm surges and waves, barrier islands, wetlands, freshwater supplies, and wildlife habitats. The Planning Tool also considers the impacts of projects and alternatives on 11 additional decision criteria, such as support of navigation, use of natural processes, flood protection of strategic assets, and support of cultural heritage.

The Planning Tool was designed to support a *deliberation-with-analysis process* by which quantitative analysis is used to frame and illuminate key policy trade-offs (National Research Council, 2009). Specifically, the Planning Tool is built around the concept of Robust Decision Making (RDM), a quantitative, deliberative approach for developing and evaluating long-term policies or strategies (Groves and Lempert, 2007; Lempert et al., 2006; Lempert, Popper, and Bankes, 2003). Communities, organizations, and governments have used RDM-based approaches to build strategies and policies that are "robust," that is, strategies that are capable of performing sufficiently well over a wide range of futures. No single strategy or policy is offered by RDM; instead, RDM helps decisionmakers to understand which strategies are the most adaptive and can evolve to meet changing conditions. Understanding which group of projects will perform best under a variety of circumstances is ultimately cost-effective, as there may be less chance that resources will be directed toward solutions that will not perform over the long run. Appendix A and the Robust Decision Making Lab (RDMlab) website (RAND Corporation, 2014) provide more information on RDM.

The Planning Tool brings together two key methodologies. The first is *quantitative decision analysis* that compares options and develops different alternatives to achieve CPRA's goals using optimization. For a specific set of goals or objectives; constraints, such as available funding; and future conditions, such as sea-level rise, the Planning Tool suggests a sequence of projects that will best meet CPRA's goals. The second is *interactive visualization*. This capability supported an iterative process in which the Planning Tool first developed proposed alternatives and estimated their effects, and then CPRA stakeholders reviewed and interacted with these results through computer visualizations to gain understanding of trade-offs. The stakeholders could then provide new goals or constraints that would be used by the Planning Tool to develop new alternatives.

The Planning Tool helped CPRA develop a consistent, scientific base of information to support four sets of deliberations leading to the final Master Plan:

1. *Comparison of individual risk-reduction and restoration projects:* Which flood risk-reduction and restoration projects are most consistent with the objectives of the Master Plan?
2. *Formulation of alternatives:* What alternatives (made up of groups of individual projects) can be implemented over a 50-year period to best achieve the objectives of the Master Plan, given constraints on funding, sediment resources, and river flow?
3. *Comparison of alternatives:* When compared across all the objectives of the Master Plan, which alternative is preferred?
4. *Evaluation of the Master Plan under uncertainty:* How will the Master Plan perform, relative to its objectives, across several future scenarios?

The Planning Tool compared the cost-effectiveness of hundreds of different proposed protection and restoration projects using estimates of project effects from the systems models. The Planning Tool was programmed to rank projects by cost-effectiveness in terms of flood risk-reduction, land building, impacts on ecosystem metrics such as fish habitat, and other decision criteria such as effects on navigation. Different rankings were calculated for the different scenarios.

The projects evaluated by the systems models and incorporated into the Planning Tool were classified into 11 different types, as shown in Figure 2.3.[3]

Figure 2.3
Large Number of Risk-Reduction and Restoration Projects Evaluated

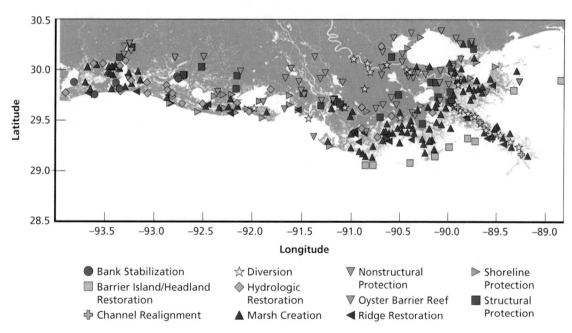

---

[3] All projects considered and their inclusion criteria are presented in Appendix A of the Master Plan (Coastal Protection and Restoration Authority of Louisiana, 2012b).

Restoration projects restore damaged or degraded parts of the coastal ecosystem through mechanical means and natural processes. There were nine different types of restoration projects considered. Bank stabilization projects reduce wave energy and prevent erosion by adding earthen fill and vegetation at the waterline of navigation channels, open bays, lakes, and bayous; ridge restoration projects use similar methods to protect existing basin ridges. Barrier island projects restore or bolster offshore islands. Sediment diversion, channel realignment, and hydrologic restoration projects manage the conveyance of sediment and river water, as well as control the intrusion of salt water into fresh areas. Other restoration projects create new marshland by piping sediment, establish oyster barrier reefs to both improve oyster cultivation and act as breakwaters against incoming surge, and protect shoreline features by installing rock barriers. In developing the final Master Plan, 248 restoration projects were considered.

Structural risk-reduction projects reduce hurricane flood risk by forming a physical barrier against a storm surge. Among this group are proposals to construct new levee and floodwall alignments; other projects would raise or otherwise augment existing levees. Thirty-three of these projects were considered.

Nonstructural risk-reduction projects reduce the vulnerability of an area to flooding without altering the flood levels themselves. They reduce hurricane flood risk in various ways and can vary among different communities, neighborhoods, and even homes. The final list of these projects evaluated included parish or sub-parish programs to elevate residential structures to a specific height above the FEMA base flood elevation, floodproof some residences and commercial properties, or implement a voluntary buyout program for residential and commercial properties facing extreme flood risk. There were 112 of these projects considered in the final evaluation.

In another mode of operation, the Planning Tool uses optimization techniques to formulate alternatives. Specifically, the Planning Tool calculates which projects would best achieve CPRA's risk-reduction and land building goals in the near and long terms, taking into account available funding over time, sediment for construction, and river flow for diversions. The Planning Tool can also develop alternatives that would maximize risk reduction and land building while meeting other specified objectives. Finally, the Planning Tool formulates unique alternatives for different scenarios, allowing CPRA to understand which projects are likely to be beneficial under most or all scenarios and which projects are beneficial for only some scenarios.

Supporting CPRA Decisionmaking with Analysis

CPRA's decisions were informed by and ultimately based on this comprehensive analytic framework. The set of interconnected systems models, including CLARA, evaluated the performance of each of the projects, using the best technical information available at that time and assuming that projects would be implemented and perform as intended. The Planning Tool then translated the output of these models to show the real-world implications of the models' data, and to systematically demonstrate (1) how projects would perform under the different scenarios in different time periods, (2) how they could help achieve CPRA's broad objectives when implemented in combination as alternatives, (3) how alternatives would differ under different funding assumptions, and (4) which alternatives would best support CPRA and stakeholder values and preferences.

Figure 2.4
Analysis Supported Stakeholder Discussions over Trade-Offs

SOURCE: CPRA, 2012a, p. 93.
NOTE: Photograph depicts a stakeholder meeting supported by CPRA Planning Tool analysis.
RAND *RR437-2.4*

The Planning Tool presents all results in an interactive visualization environment, with views customized to address different planning questions, as described in the next chapter.

In the next chapter, we discuss how CPRA used the Planning Tool to evaluate and compare different alternatives and their trade-off analysis. We then briefly describe the final decisions that are the foundation of the comprehensive final Master Plan.

CHAPTER THREE

Using the Planning Tool to Support the Development of a Comprehensive Plan for Louisiana

CPRA used the Planning Tool to support an iterative participatory process to decide which group of projects should form the basis of Louisiana's $50 billion plan. Here, we describe the way in which the Planning Tool was used to compare projects using a common approach, to develop and compare a wide array of project groupings, or alternatives, and to understand the performance, environmental, and policy trade-offs among them.

It is important to note that the Planning Tool was not used to tell CPRA which alternative to choose. Rather, it supported an informed dialogue with coastal Louisiana stakeholders. To decide on a final Master Plan, CPRA considered input from stakeholders and management on the trade-offs needed to appreciate the implications of trying to balance multiple decision criteria relative to the ultimate goal of landscape sustainability. The results from the final analysis of the Master Plan are presented, using the 50-year time horizon assumed for the Plan.

Planning Tool Analysis Supported Deliberations

Comparing Projects on an Even Playing Field

Early in the planning process, CPRA decided that it needed to evaluate the large list of projects that had been proposed over the preceding several decades using a consistent methodology, data, and set of models. This information, it was believed, would help CPRA focus on the most promising projects and provide the needed information to set aside less-attractive options.

The CPRA systems models and Planning Tool, therefore, were first used to evaluate how individual projects might affect the coast over 50 years, with respect to the primary goals of reducing risk and building land across the scenarios. As described in Chapter Two, CPRA evaluated 393 risk-reduction and restoration project concepts: 248 restoration projects, 33 structural risk-reduction projects, and 112 nonstructural risk-reduction projects. Interactive visualizations were developed to show how different projects ranked based on cost-effectiveness. This information supported early stakeholder workshops that helping build confidence in the data and tools being used, and laid the foundation for proposed alternatives that would include only the best options.

Determining How To Allocate Funds Across Project Types

The next step to developing the plan was to consider how big of a plan to create and how to allocate funding between risk-reduction projects and restoration projects. The size of the plan would depend on how much funding from different state and federal sources would be available. This was a big uncertainty. Therefore, CPRA drew from documents such as the 2007 Master Plan and previous related legislation for estimates, and considered new revenue, such as funds coming from penalties and claims arising from the BP *Deepwater Horizon* oil spill, where appropriate. The list of future funding considered in the planning stage is presented in Appendix B of the Master Plan (Coastal Protection and Restoration Authority of Louisiana, 2012b). This analysis suggested a range of plausible funding levels between $20 billion and $50 billion over the 50-year planning horizon.

CPRA next used the Planning Tool to estimate how much land and how much risk reduction plans of various sizes would provide. The Planning Tool was used to generate 25 alternatives that varied total funding between $20 billion and $100 billion and allocations between 30-percent risk-reduction projects and 70-percent restoration projects (30/70) to 70-percent risk-reduction projects and 30-percent restoration projects (70/30). Alternatives were developed for two of the three environmental scenarios described in Chapter Two.

Figure 3.1. shows results for long-term risk reduction and land building when equally weighting near-term and long-term benefits for the moderate scenario. Each colored line represents a fixed level of funding and traces out how the land building and risk-reduction performance changes as the funding mix is shifted from mostly risk-reduction projects (points labeled 30%/70%) to mostly restoration projects (70%/30% splits).

Increasing the total funding level leads, as expected, to higher risk reduction and a greater amount of land built; the trade-off lines shift to the upper right. Similarly, increasing the proportion of funding earmarked for risk reduction increased the long-term risk-reduction performance, at the expense of long-term land building. Results with different emphases on near-term and long-term benefits showed similar patterns.

Figure 3.1
Trade-Offs Between Land Building and Risk Reduction for Different Amounts and Allocations of Funding

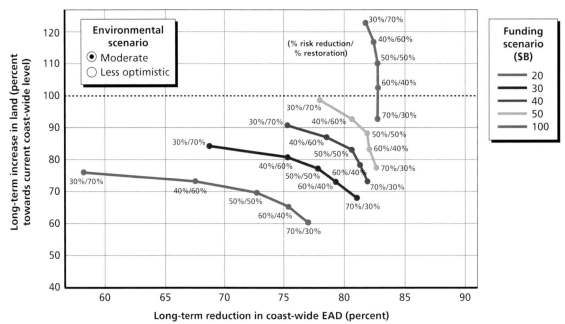

SOURCE: RAND analysis.

One noteworthy result is that, regardless of the funding level, it was impossible to reduce the long-term EAD by more than about 83 percent of the current level using the projects proposed for inclusion in the Master Plan. Even with a total budget of $100 billion, some residual risk remains. Figure 3.1 clearly illustrates that, beyond a certain point, devoting further resources to risk reduction has little additional benefit and imposes a significant decrease in land building capacity—at least for the projects conceptualized to date.

This is an example of the kind of trade-off exercise that the Master Plan Delivery Team walked through with CPRA and its stakeholders to arrive at a final plan that balances the marginal benefit of shifting funds from one project type to another.

Striking a Balance Between Near-Term and Long-Term Outcomes

In order to use the Planning Tool to develop alternatives that would achieve CPRA's goals, CPRA needed to also determine how to balance near-term and long-term progress. CPRA used the Planning Tool to calculate ten alternatives that incrementally varied this balance between 0 percent near-term/100 percent long-term and 90 percent near-term/10 percent long-term. Each alternative was based on a total $50 billion, 50-year budget, split equally between risk-reduction projects and restoration projects.

By using the analysis of near-term and long-term trade-offs in performance generated by the Planning Tool, CPRA ended up choosing a 50-percent near-term and 50-percent long-term approach that balances the need to respond with urgency to the coastal crisis while investing in long-term solutions.

Balancing Among Different Planning Objectives

CPRA was charged not only to reduce risk and build land, but also ensure that the other objectives—such as providing habitats to support an array of commercial and recreational activities coast-wide—were met. For example, building land can, over the long term, decrease the salinity of shallow wetlands where shrimp and other aquatic species spend parts of their lives.

CPRA used the Planning Tool to perform a series of sensitivity analyses on how alternatives could be modified so that ecosystem and other coastal objectives were met (Groves and Sharon, 2013). As an example, Figure 3.2 shows the trade-offs between land area built by year 50 and constraints on the minimum habitat outcomes for some shrimp and saltwater fisheries, respectively. The "without action" alternative results in the significant loss of about 700 square miles and shows a slight increase in the saltwater species habitat. The "maximize land building" alternative, conversely, leads to stabilization of coast-wide land area over time but would lead to a significant decline in the saltwater species' habitat.

Because prevention of land loss was one of the state's primary objectives, this weighed more heavily in the development of the final Master Plan alternative, but this is an example of the trade-offs considered between a primary metric and the consequent impacts on ecosystem services like shrimp habitat.

Ensuring Robustness for the Uncertain Future

The projects selected for inclusion in an alternative by the Planning Tool also differed depending on which environmental scenario was evaluated. The set of projects that maximize land building in the moderate scenario, for example, was different from those projects that maximize land building under the less optimistic scenario. As more scenarios are evaluated in subsequent analyses, additional trade-offs will likely emerge.

Figure 3.2
Trade-Offs Between Land Building and Area of Suitable Saltwater Habitat

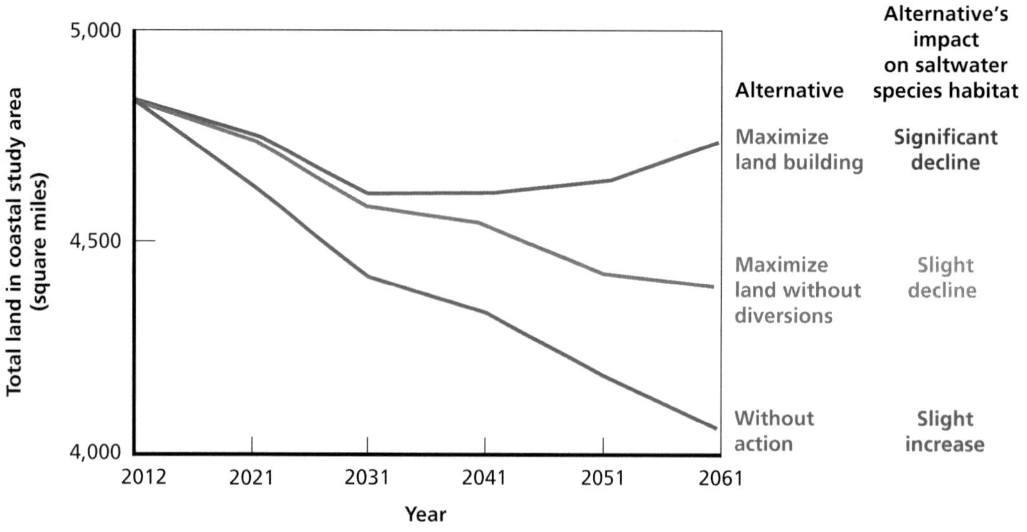

SOURCE: Groves, Fischbach, Knopman, et al., 2013.
RAND *RR437-3.2*

CPRA found that restoration projects selected under less optimistic conditions tended to be in the upper end of the estuaries, closer to existing land, than projects close to the Gulf of Mexico. Informed by these results, CPRA chose to base the Master Plan on the projects selected under the less optimistic scenario. This alternative will perform slightly less well than others under moderate conditions but will have greater benefits if conditions similar to the less optimistic scenario come to pass. Adjustments to the investments specified to occur in later decades will likely be needed as the Master Plan is stress tested under a broader range of future scenarios and as experience is gained and expectations adjusted based on implementation of near-term projects.

Louisiana's 2012 Comprehensive Master Plan for a Sustainable Coast

CPRA reviewed trade-offs among alternatives by looking at how results for long-term risk reduction and land building changed and how project selection varied under the range of constraints. Using this information, CPRA identified threshold values (in terms of a minimum acceptable outcome) for some decision criteria and sought judgment by stakeholders and other experts about different projects to include or exclude in the final plan (Groves, Sharon, and Knopman, 2012). After several months of discussions among CPRA management and stakeholders and iterations with the Planning Tool, CPRA defined a single alternative for the January 2012 draft of the Master Plan (Coastal Protection and Restoration Authority of Louisiana, 2012a). The draft 2012 coastal Master Plan was released on January 12, 2012, for public review and comment. CPRA held three all-day public meetings and more than 50 meetings with community groups, parish officials, legislators, and stakeholder groups. Thousands of comments were received and reviewed and some of the underlying information on the individual projects was updated for accuracy.

The Planning Tool was used again to evaluate how adjustments to the included projects and their implementation timing would change final outcomes. Based on a review of this new analysis, refinements were made and the final Master Plan was completed. The Louisiana legislature subsequently approved the final Master Plan unanimously in May 2012.

Figures 3.3 to 3.6 summarize key decisions and final outcomes of the Master Plan. Figure 3.3 shows how Master Plan funding is allocated across different project types and the number of projects for each type; 109 projects are included in the final alternative. Notably, about 20 percent of the total funding ($10.9 billion) is allocated to nonstructural risk-reduction projects coast-wide and $4 billion of funding is allocated to 11 different sediment-diversion projects.

Figure 3.4 shows that the implementation of the Master Plan is projected to dramatically decrease EAD from coast-wide flooding, from a currently estimated annual level of $2.2 billion today to between $2.8 billion and $4.8 billion in year 50 with the full implementation of the Master Plan. Without the Master Plan in place, EAD could exceed $20 billion under the less optimistic scenario.

Figure 3.5 graphically illustrates this flood risk reduction under the less optimistic scenario assumptions by showing the change in future 100-year flood depths—or flood depths that would have a 1-percent chance of occurring in any year—with the Master Plan in place, as compared to a future without action. Like Figure 1.3, the areas marked in blue face deeper levels of flooding; areas marked in orange face less flooding. Of note are the dramatically reduced flood depths projected in New Orleans, a result of several upgrades to the existing system (itself substantially upgraded since Hurricane Katrina). The extensive construction of new levees over broad areas of the central coast could also provide substantial flood depth reduction of between four and 12 feet for 1-percent AEP events, given the assumptions of the less optimistic scenario.

Compared to the future without action, the restoration projects included in the Master Plan could build between 580 and 800 square miles of land over the next 50 years, depending on future conditions, as illustrated in Figure 3.6. For the moderate scenario, land loss would be

Figure 3.3
Master Plan Funding Allocation Across Project Types

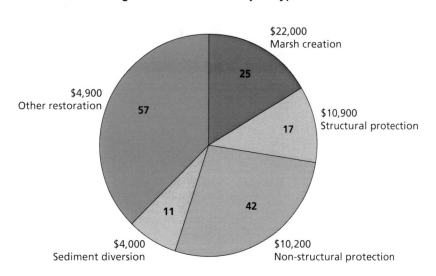

SOURCE: Groves, Sharon, and Knopman, 2012, Figure 4.17.
NOTE: Indicated values are in millions of 2010 U.S. dollars.
RAND RR437-3.3

Figure 3.4
Reduction in Coast-Wide Risk With and Without the Master Plan

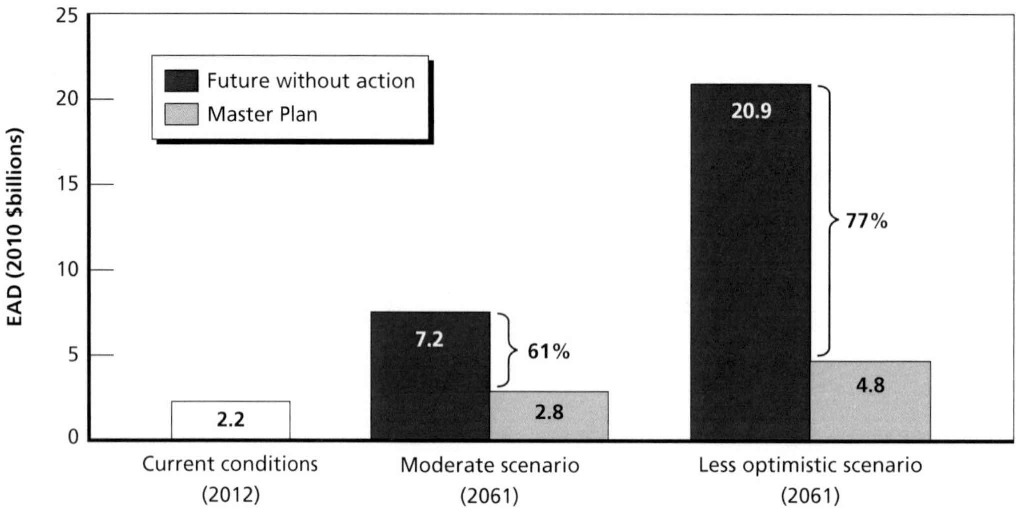

SOURCE: Groves, Fischbach, Knopman, et al., 2013.
RAND *RR437-3.4*

halted in about 20 years and begin increasing for the next 30 years. For the less optimistic scenario, land loss would still continue but at about half the rate as without the Master Plan. If future conditions are more like those represented by the less optimistic scenario, additional investments would need to be made to stabilize land area.

Next Steps for Louisiana

The final 2012 Master Plan presents a large-scale, comprehensive risk-reduction and restoration strategy for the Louisiana coast. One and a half years since its adoption by the Louisiana legislature, the state has begun moving ahead with the implementation of near-term projects and the development of new data and tools to refine the plan in the coming years.

For the state's fiscal year ending in June 2013, Louisiana was projected to spend about $526 million to support projects in different stages of implementation: planning (12 projects; $19 million); design and engineering (31 projects; $41 million); construction (53 projects; $451 million); and operations, maintenance, and monitoring (89 projects; $16 million) (Coastal Protection and Restoration Authority of Louisiana, 2012a). In FY14, CPRA expects to spend about $725 million on over 50 projects consistent with the Master Plan (Coastal Protection and Restoration Authority, 2013).

CPRA has also been working to refine the Master Plan to support its implementation and adapt as improved information becomes available. This refinement is entirely consistent with the planning framework developed for the 2012 Master Plan. CPRA also will continue to use updated and refined systems models, including CLARA, and the Planning Tool.

An important area of refinement is the nonstructural component of the Master Plan. The final Master Plan specified that over $10 billion be spent over the coming decades on nonstructural risk mitigation. The new Coastal Community Resiliency Program will help develop

Figure 3.5
Reduction in 100-Year Flood Depths in 50 Years Due to Master Plan (Less Optimistic Scenario)

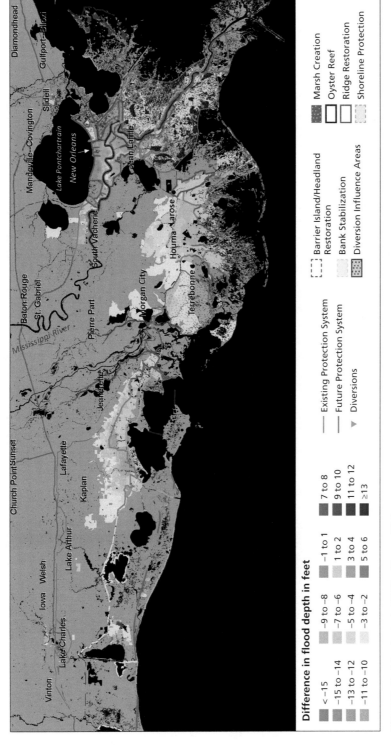

SOURCE: Fischbach et al., 2012a, Figure 10.6.
RAND RR437-3.5

Figure 3.6
Change in Land Area With and Without Master Plan

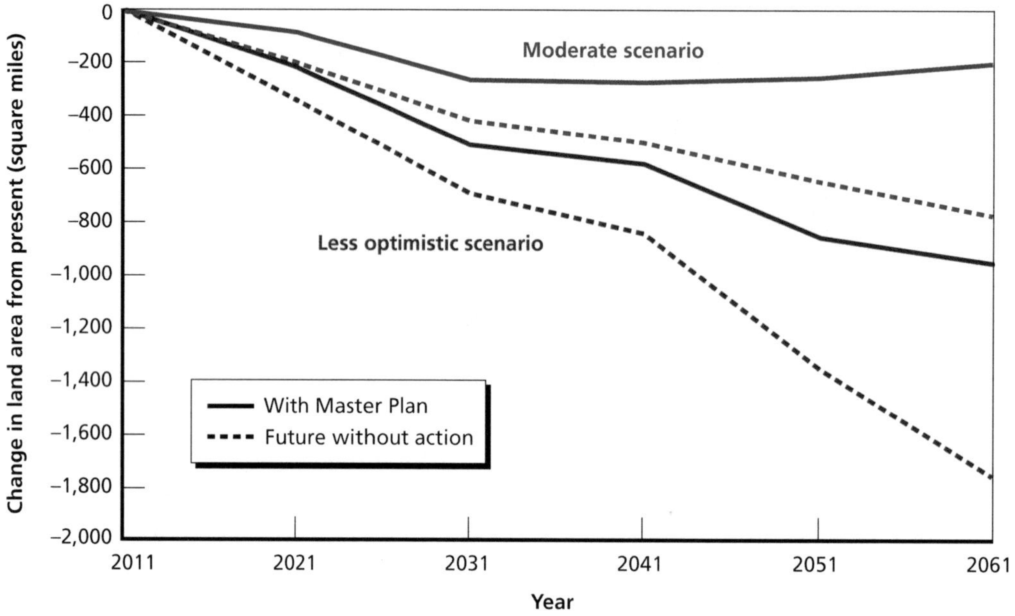

SOURCE: Groves, Sharon, and Knopman, 2012, Figures S.5 and S.6.
RAND *RR437-3.6*

improved data and tools and obtain stakeholder input so that $10 billion in spending can be targeted both to the areas in most critical need and in ways that are most complementary to existing and planned structural protection infrastructure. The state has also initiated a new collaboration with the U.S. Army Corps of Engineers to determine how best to reconnect the Mississippi River to adjacent basins and to ascertain how much sediment and water carried by the river system can be used for wetland restoration (Schleifstein, 2013). Other programs have also been started to improve monitoring of existing and future restoration efforts and refine scientific understanding of the physical processes governing the evolution of the coastal landscape.

Armed with new tools, scientific information, and public input, CPRA, stakeholders, and coastal scientists will begin work in 2014 to refine the Master Plan for the 2017 update. This process should lead to the first of many required adjustments to the current 50-year plan over the coming decades. Only with diligent monitoring and adaptation, and learning from experience gained from implementation of near-term projects, will the desired outcomes of the 2012 Master Plan be realized over the coming decades.

CHAPTER FOUR

Reducing Coastal Risk Through Integrated Planning

Louisiana is not alone. Its hard-earned experience and path forward offer valuable insights to coastal regions everywhere. In this chapter, we offer a brief summary of the scale of the coastal flooding problem across the United States and then draw out key elements of Louisiana's response, as embodied in its ongoing planning and implementation processes, that have relevance to many other places. We conclude by highlighting the key features of a comprehensive approach to coastal planning that incorporates the principles of deliberation with analysis along with early, sustained, and transparent stakeholder and decisionmaker engagement.

Growing Vulnerability of Coastal Regions

According to the U.S. Census Bureau, the populations of U.S. coastal counties have grown by more than 45 percent between 1970 and 2010, amounting to 50 million new coastal residents and billions of dollars in additional assets (homes and businesses) in these areas (National Climatic Data Center, 2012). Concurrently, coastal disaster losses have grown in the United States along its more than 95,000 miles of coastline. While some years pass without a hurricane landfall, in other years, the country sees substantial hurricane activity. In just the 2004, 2005, and 2008 hurricane seasons, for example, six or more hurricanes caused significant damage in the United States. Large storms that hit vulnerable and high-asset-value parts of the coastline, such as Katrina and Sandy, have caused more damage than the total inflation-adjusted losses from all hurricanes in the 1960s, 1970s, and 1980s combined (Collins and Lowe, 2001; Pielke and Landsea, 1998). In 2012 alone, there were 11 different climate or weather-related disasters that each caused at least $1 billion in damage, with the total exceeding $110 billion (National Climatic Data Center, 2012).

While each coastal region faces a combination of risks that is as unique as the location itself, the vulnerabilities stem from a number of common factors:

- **Unpredictable natural events and human activities,** such as coastal storms, changing climate conditions, landscape processes, and economic development in the coastal zone.
- **Diverse uses of the "at-risk" zone,** including residency, agriculture, commercial and recreational fishing, and in some cases, oil and gas extraction, place demands on natural resources that may run counter to sustainable risk-management practices.
- **Fragile ecosystems,** such as estuaries, wetlands, mudflats, and mangrove forests provide a buffer zone between storm surge and human development, but they are at risk of collapse from saltwater intrusion, erosion, and other natural forces.

A recent study by Hallegatte, Green, Nicholls, and Corfee-Morlot (2013) estimates that eight of the 20 most vulnerable cities in the world in terms of annual average loss from coastal flooding are located in the United States (Figure 4.1). New York, Miami, and New Orleans are most at risk in terms of EAD. While much of the risk stems from the higher value of assets in developed countries like the United States, Hallegatte et al. (2013) notes that flood risk management in the United States is generally more reliant on flood warning and evacuation than formal flood defenses when compared to many European and Asian cities.

Hurricane Sandy is a case in point. In October 2012, Sandy dealt a major blow to the mid-Atlantic region, particularly coastal New York and New Jersey. The storm flooded train and subway tunnels, damaged electric power transmission and distribution equipment, damaged or destroyed 650,000 homes and businesses, caused at least 165 fatalities, and is estimated to have resulted in economic losses of $50 billion (NYC Special Initiative for Rebuilding and Resiliency, 2013; Donovan, 2013).

Figure 4.1
Cities with the Highest Risks of Coastal Flooding, 2005

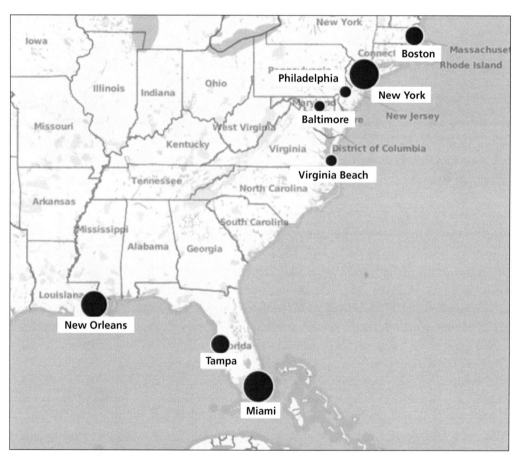

SOURCE: RAND analysis using data from Hallegatte, Green, Nicholls, and Corfee-Morlot, 2013.
NOTE: The size of the symbols represents relative annual risks, ranging from $76M/year for Baltimore to $672M/year for Miami. Risk estimates assume assets and flood protection as of 2005.
RAND RR437-4.1

Costs of Coastal Flooding

Governmental spending on disaster recovery has been rising along with increasing storm damage. Looking at just the allocations for the two largest budget items—FEMA's Disaster Relief Fund, and the Federal Housing Administration's Emergency Response budget—the steady increase over the last four decades is evident (Figure 4.2). Of course, this total captures only the federal government's portion of disaster relief spending, while the costs borne by homeowners, businesses, state and local governments, and others make the total much larger.

Whether insured losses or not, many of these costs could be avoided with better planning and investments in mitigation or resilience before storms arrive. Recent estimates suggest that the United States is substantially under-investing in pre-disaster mitigation. For example, one study suggests that the gap between mitigation investment and expected disaster assistance costs could run as high as $1.2 to $7.1 trillion over the next 75 years (Cummins, Suher, and Zanjani, 2010). Meanwhile, the payoff for disaster risk mitigation—the ratio of benefits to costs for each additional dollar spent on mitigation—has been estimated to be between 4:1 and 15:1 (Godschalk et al., 2009; Healy and Malhotra, 2009; Multihazard Mitigation Council, 2005).

The many risks from coastal storms are expected to increase due to the continued aggregation of people and wealth on our coasts, coupled with the effects of global climate change. In turn, however, the potential benefits from risk-reduction investment could also rise in the future. As the U.S. taxpayer increasingly becomes the insurer of last resort for coastal residents, there is a strong need to carefully consider near-term investments in coastal infrastructure, res-

Figure 4.2
Hurricane Flood Damages and Federal Disaster Recovery Expenditures, 1970–2013 (Constant 2013 U.S. Dollars)

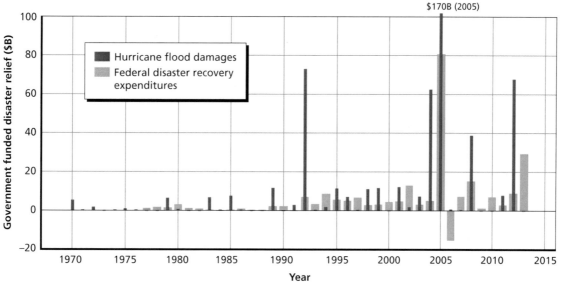

SOURCE: RAND analysis.
NOTE: The negative expenditure in 2006 represents funds rescinded from previous (cumulative) appropriations via the "Omnibus Consolidated Rescissions and Appropriations Act of 1996." While some funds were allocated in that bill to other expenses relating to disasters, the overall appropriation for the disaster relief fund was decreased.
RAND RR437-4.2

toration, and disaster risk mitigation to help reduce the long-term national liability for these risks.

Strengthening Coastal Resilience Requires a Comprehensive Planning Process

Increasingly, coastal states and regions in the United States and elsewhere in the world are recognizing the need to take a more comprehensive and coordinated approach to managing risk and developing coastal resilience. The challenges facing other coastal regions are similar to those that are faced by Louisiana.

Coastal Risks Are Increasing, but in Uncertain Ways

Tropical storms and hurricanes alone have always had the potential to cause damaging floods. Human population density and development patterns exacerbate the risk, as do the changes made to the coastal environment to support local communities and industry. Climate change, which is increasing sea levels in most places and could be influencing the frequency or severity of large tropical storms, will increase the risk of flooding over time for many coastal regions, but with uncertain timing and magnitude. For long-term planning, this type of uncertainty is "deep," as there is often no consensus on the best model for estimating what may happen or for assigning likelihoods of different plausible outcomes (Lempert, Popper, and Bankes, 2003).

Deep uncertainty can be particularly confounding to sustainable planning and decisionmaking. Although scientists can develop a wide range of credible estimates of how factors affecting coastal conditions could change, any single prediction of the future could be significantly off. Disagreements about which prediction on which to base a long-term plan can consume considerable amounts of energy and time, without clear value in the end. As described below, when researchers cannot predict the future with sufficient accuracy, planners are typically better off understanding under which conditions plans would perform poorly and developing alternatives that are robust to these vulnerabilities.

There Are Many Different Types of Strategies to Consider to Reduce Risks and Restore Coastal Landscapes

Traditionally, flood management has been addressed through structural solutions, including constructing levees to hold floodwaters back, channelizing and dredging rivers to speed up flows and reduce flooding of banks, and hardening of shorelines through rock and concrete. Similarly, many approaches to ecosystem restoration rely on mechanical means—such as moving dirt to rebuild eroded wetlands or replacing sand that has been washed away. More recently, however, nonstructural and less mechanical solutions are being considered for both flood-risk reduction and ecosystem restoration. Damage from flooding, for example, can be reduced by elevating or floodproofing structures. Natural landscapes can be restored and maintained by reintroducing natural hydrologic processes that bring silt-laden floodwaters to areas adjacent to rivers. The Louisiana Master Plan evaluated and included a diverse set of different types of projects.

These options not only operate in fundamentally different ways, but also have different effects on risk reduction, land loss, and ecological functions—positive and negative. Traditional evaluations based on present-value costs and monetized benefits may not capture the important differences among different strategies. Local residents and the nation receive substantial benefits from a healthy and productive coastal ecosystem, but these "ecosystem service" benefits have only recently been recognized as goals for future planning. They remain difficult to measure and quantify. Further, scientific understanding of these benefits, or how ecosystem services can be sustained alongside economic development, remains incomplete. We also lack the tools to fully comprehend how different coastal ecosystems can help to reduce the power of storm surge or waves before they reach homes and communities.

A successful planning approach will need to address many different types of solutions and do so in a technically credible and balanced way.

Solutions Will Be Implemented by Local, Regional, State, and Federal Agencies

Coastal floods and flood risk affect large coastal regions, with impacts that often cross municipal, state, or national borders. Investments made to reduce risk by one community without coordinated action—for example, constructing a new levee or floodwall—could simply shift the water and risk into other territories. Similarly, flood-risk reduction investments in one area can negatively impact the environmental conditions and ecosystem services of another.

Regional plans will be necessary to help reconcile conflicts at the local level, allocate resources more efficiently to address the most salient problems, and ensure that proposed solutions align with the size and scale of the challenges addressed (Wilbanks, 2009). CPRA, for example, was formed to provide a convening and authoritative body to develop and implement Louisiana's Coastal Master Plan. In other areas, like the Hurricane Sandy–affected region, there is not yet such an entity. At the time of this writing, the Federal Hurricane Sandy Rebuilding Task Force included coordinated regional planning as a key recommendation for investment and planning in the Sandy-affected region in future years (Hurricane Sandy Rebuilding Task Force, 2013).

Principles for Integrated Coastal Planning

Given the uncertainty of how these factors—alone or in combination—will play out in a given region, coastal regions and communities are in need of a new approach to developing coastal resilience plans with actionable strategies. Our work in Louisiana and elsewhere suggests that the approach should be based on three principles:

Public Participation Is Essential Throughout the Planning Process

In coping with each of these challenges, meaningful and sustained stakeholder involvement is essential for several reasons. First, the planning team can vet analytical results with the individuals most knowledgeable about how the system operates in practice. Affected populations; civic, trade, and environmental groups; and responsible agencies can bring to light a misunderstood or neglected fundamental fact about the region or potential strategy. For example, navigation interest groups can provide important information about how projects that modify river flows could affect navigation that would not be identified by the current available suite of systems models. Additionally, stakeholders should play a meaningful role that allows them to contribute expertise and insight into the planning process. Stakeholder interests in coastal resilience plans may include marine transportation experts, environmental and wildlife advocacy groups, members of oil and gas energy sectors, marine fishery groups, homeland security agencies, tourism and recreation agencies, and others. Since every coastal plan will be as unique as the region it represents, the plan needs to reflect local needs and understanding.

Second, the planning process should be participatory and involve collective problem recognition and problem solving to ensure that reasonable concerns and solutions from the full range of stakeholders are considered. Without this participation, an otherwise technically sound planning process and plan can be derailed and implementation stalled. A comprehensive plan is the sum total of many smaller decisions regarding individual projects and choices of which to implement. There is also time-dependency among the projects: each project chosen may directly or indirectly affect the success of subsequent options.

Finally, transparency in the planning process can facilitate greater public trust and buy-in of the final plan. Further, open and timely communication with the public and stakeholders will empower everyone to understand what needs to be done as plans are put into action.

Technical Analysis Is Meant to Inform Deliberations and Value Judgments by Decisionmakers

Decisionmakers involved in creating a comprehensive coastal plan will be faced with many difficult choices. They will need to take social, economic, and ecological concerns into consideration. These are value judgments, not technical choices per se. At its best, scientific data and analysis should make apparent these trade-offs and inform the deliberative process. These deliberations should be guided by peer-reviewed scientific evidence pertaining to (1) what risks are present, (2) what risks may be imminent, and (3) what strategies are the most effective to offset those risks. The descriptor "best available" reminds us that scientific knowledge is always evolving. New data and information should be used to expand, clarify, update, or even change strategies as needed. This analysis, however, should be developed not to define a single solution, but rather support deliberations (National Research Council, 2009).

A Sustainable Long-Term Strategy Must Be Robust and Adaptive

Given the inherent uncertainty about the future and ambiguity of how different strategies will play out in the future, a comprehensive strategy for strengthening our coasts will need to be robust. A robust strategy will be one that will perform sufficiently well across a wide range of plausible futures.

Robust decision methods, including RDM, exploit increasingly capable computer tools and are well suited for such situations. RDM rests on a simple concept: Rather than using models and data to describe a best-estimate future, RDM runs models many hundreds to thousands of times to determine how plans perform in a range of plausible futures. Visualization and statistical analysis of the resulting database of runs then help decisionmakers distinguish those future conditions in which their plans perform well from those in which their plans perform poorly, assisting them in making their plans more robust.

Robust decision methods can help structure a "deliberation with analysis" process such that a robust and adaptive strategy can emerge. Appendix A of this report provides more details about RDM.

Building on Louisiana's Planning Experience

The development of the Louisiana Master Plan largely followed these three principles. It was highly participatory, engaging many different stakeholder groups throughout the year and a half of planning. The systems models, including CLARA, provided the best available scientific and engineering information about a wide range of possible projects to address Louisiana's coastal challenges. The CPRA Planning Tool then was able to distill the vast quantities of technical information into a manageable number of interactive visualizations that were used to support stakeholder and CPRA deliberations.

Finally, the resulting Comprehensive Master Plan took important steps toward establishing a robust set of investments. Recognizing the uncertainty about future flood risk, a significant portion (20 percent) of the $50 billion budget is to be allocated to nonstructural risk-reduction strategies. These strategies will be developed over time, allowing CPRA to benefit both from observing how risks are evolving over the coming decades and from new scientific advancements and understanding. Other ways that the Master Plan is designed to be robust is the use of river- and sediment-diversion projects as a means to restore and sustain wetlands. These projects will be fine-tuned over the coming decades to maximize the long-term land building effects while managing the accompanying but temporary environmental changes.

These principles, demonstrated by the Louisiana Comprehensive Master Planning process, can provide a template for coastal sustainability planning in other regions. Investments made in coastal resilience planning and subsequent policies and actions may offset the risks associated with storm surge flooding, and thus pay for themselves through reduced future damage. The tragic and costly events of the recent years—including hurricanes Katrina, Rita, and Sandy—have demonstrated that our coastal cities face unacceptably high risk and rapidly degrading coastal ecosystems. The best available science suggests that these risks and impacts will only grow over time without significant investments in coastal resilience. Although the future is uncertain, the time is now to develop and implement smart, comprehensive plans for coastal resilience.

APPENDIX

A Brief Description of Robust Decision Making

The planning framework used to support the development of *Louisiana's Comprehensive Master Plan for a Sustainable Coast* (Coastal Protection and Restoration Authority of Louisiana, 2012a) incorporated many of the principles of Robust Decision Making (RDM)—a decisionmaking method that provides a systematic and objective approach for developing management strategies that are more robust to uncertainty about the future (Groves and Lempert, 2007; Lempert, Popper, and Bankes, 2003). This approach has been used in many long-term planning applications, including water resources management, energy resources, and national security (Groves, Fischbach, Bloom, et al., 2013; Dixon, Lempert, LaTourrette, and Reville, 2007; Lempert and Groves, 2010; Popper et al., 2009). When applied to natural resources planning, RDM helps planners iteratively identify and evaluate robust strategies—those that perform well in terms of management objectives over a wide range of plausible futures but that may perform less well under an assumption that one future may be most likely to occur. Trading off optimality for adequacy across many possible conditions is referred to as "satisficing" (Simon, 1956).

Often, the robust strategies identified using RDM are adaptive (as opposed to static), meaning that they are designed to evolve over time in response to new information. RDM helps decisionmakers identify strategies—including both near-term and deferred decisions or investments—that are shown through the analysis to be effective over a wide range of plausible future conditions. RDM also can be used to facilitate group decisionmaking in contentious situations where parties to the decision have strong disagreements about assumptions and values (Groves and Lempert, 2007; Lempert et al., 2006; Lempert and Popper, 2005).

The engine that makes RDM run is a sophisticated set of statistical and software tools embedded in a process of participatory stakeholder engagement. RDM helps resource managers develop adaptive strategies by iteratively evaluating the performance of proposed options against a wide array of plausible futures, systematically identifying the key vulnerabilities of those strategies,[1] and using this information to suggest responses to the vulnerabilities identified (Lempert and Collins, 2007; Lempert, Popper, and Bankes, 2003; Means et al., 2010). Successive iterations develop and refine strategies that are increasingly robust. Final decisions among strategies are made by considering a few robust choices and weighing their remaining vulnerabilities.

RDM follows an iterative and interactive series of steps consistent with the "deliberation with analysis" decision support process described by the National Research Council (2009) (Figure A.1). These steps are summarized below.

---

[1] The approach to identifying key vulnerabilities uses statistical "scenario discovery" algorithms (Bryant and Lempert, 2010; Groves and Lempert, 2007). The terms "scenario discovery" and "vulnerability analysis" are synonymous.

Figure A.1
Iterative Steps to a Robust Decision Making Analysis

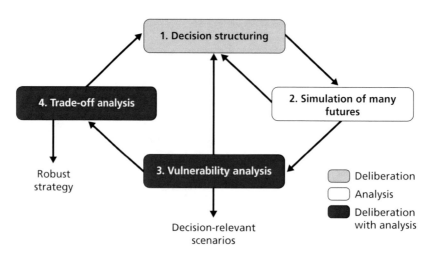

SOURCE: Groves, Fischbach, Bloom, et al., 2013, Figure 2.2.
RAND *RR437-A.1*

1. **Decision structuring:** The process begins with a deliberation step in which decision-makers, experts, agency professionals, members of the public, and other stakeholders work together to define the scope of the planning process. This includes identifying key goals and objectives; defining the critical uncertain factors that could influence future planning conditions and the success of different strategies; developing a preliminary set of options or strategy to evaluate; defining performance metrics that will be used to assess how different strategies might perform across plausible futures; and compiling data and developing models to estimate how different strategies would perform, relative to the metrics, across the plausible futures.

2. **Simulation of many futures:** The second step is an analysis step in which the inputs developed in the decision-structuring step are used along with data and models to evaluate plausible future conditions across a wide range of futures for one or more strategies. This step generates a significant amount of quantitative information, generally stored in a database, that is next used to understand under which conditions one or more strategies do not meet the stated goals and objectives of the planning process.

3. **Vulnerability analysis:** In this step, decisionmakers and stakeholders work together to define a few key scenarios that describe conditions to which the strategies evaluated in step 2 are most vulnerable and thus relevant to the decisionmaking. This is supported by statistical analysis and interactive visualizations. It is not necessary that decision-makers and stakeholders reach agreement about how likely these strategies are. Instead, this process provides information that can be used to refine the strategies considered—returning to step 1—or evaluate the important trade-offs among strategies in step 4.

4. **Trade-off analysis:** The fourth step also uses the analysis from the previous steps to support a deliberation over strategies. To support this, analysts develop interactive visualizations that highlight the key trade-offs among different strategies and their performance across the different futures, including the scenarios that illuminate the key vulnerabilities. At this point in the process, additional scientific information and expert

judgment can be incorporated to provide context about the likelihoods of the key scenarios, and stakeholder preferences about different outcomes can be considered along with the analytic results to help inform the selection of a robust strategy. In many cases, these deliberations identify a strategy that is preliminary and contains elements that need further evaluation, refinement, or augmentation. This preliminary robust strategy can then be used as a new starting point for additional iterations through the process. In this way, RDM helps support an ongoing, iterative planning process that can accompany the implementation over time of large and potentially costly strategies.

RDM continues to evolve and improve as experience is gained across a broad range of applications. The website for RAND's Robust Decision Making Lab (RAND Corporation, 2014) provides summaries and links to the key methodological studies and descriptions as well as links to RDM applications in various planning sectors by researchers across a growing network of institutions.

References

Brinkley, Douglas, *The Great Deluge: Hurricane Katrina, New Orleans, and the Mississippi Gulf Coast*, New York: HarperCollins, 2006.

Bryant, Benjamin P., and Robert J. Lempert, "Thinking Inside the Box: A Participatory, Computer-Assisted Approach to Scenario Discovery," *Technological Forecasting and Social Change*, Vol. 77, No. 1, 2010, pp. 34–49.

Coastal Protection and Restoration Authority, *Fiscal Year 2014 Annual Plan: Integrated Ecosystem Restoration and Hurricane Protection in Coastal Louisiana*, Baton Rouge, La., 2013. As of September 26, 2013:
http://www.lacpra.org/assets/docs/fy2014AnnualPlanWeb.pdf

Coastal Protection and Restoration Authority of Louisiana, *Integrated Ecosystem Restoration and Hurricane Protection: Louisiana's Comprehensive Master Plan for a Sustainable Coast*, Baton Rouge, La., February 2007.

———, *Louisiana's Comprehensive Master Plan for a Sustainable Coast*, Baton Rouge, La., 2012a. As of April 30, 2012:
http://www.coastalmasterplan.louisiana.gov/2012-master-plan/final-master-plan/

———, *Louisiana's Comprehensive Master Plan for a Sustainable Coast, Appendices A-J*, Baton Rouge, La., 2012b. As of April 30, 2012:
http://www.coastalmasterplan.louisiana.gov/2012-master-plan/master-plan-appendices/

Cobell, Zachary, Haihong Zhao, Hugh J. Roberts, F. Ryan Clark, and Shan Zou, "Surge and Wave Modeling for the Louisiana 2012 Coastal Master Plan," *Journal of Coastal Research*, No. 67, Special Issue, Summer 2013, pp. 88–108.

Collins, Douglas J., and Stephen P. Lowe, "A Macro Validation Dataset for US Hurricane Models," *Casualty Actuarial Society*, Winter Forum, 2001, pp. 217–252.

Couvillion, Brady R., John A. Barras, Gregory D. Steyer, WIlliam Sleavin, Michelle Fischer, Holly Beck, Nadine Trahan, Brad Griffin, and David Heckman, "Land Area Change in Coastal Louisiana from 1932 to 2010: U.S. Geological Survey Scientific Investigations Map 3164," pamphlet, Reston, Va.: U.S. Geological Survey, 2011. As of April 30, 2012:
http://pubs.usgs.gov/sim/3164/downloads/SIM3164_Pamphlet.pdf

Cummins, J. David, Michael Suher, and George Zanjani, "Federal Financial Exposure to Natural Catastrophe Risk," in Deborah Lucas, ed., *Measuring and Managing Federal Financial Risk*, Chicago, Ill.: University of Chicago Press, National Bureau of Economic Research, 2010, pp. 61–92. As of July 24, 2013:
http://www.nber.org/chapters/c3036

Dixon, Lloyd, Robert J. Lempert, Tom LaTourrette, and Robert T. Reville, *The Federal Role in Terrorism Insurance: Evaluating Alternatives in an Uncertain World*, Santa Monica, Calif.: RAND Corporation, MG-679-CTRMP, 2007. As of February 28, 2013:
http://www.rand.org/pubs/monographs/MG679.html

Dokka, Roy K., "Modern-Day Tectonic Subsidence in Coastal Louisiana," *Geology*, Vol. 34, No. 4, April 1, 2006, pp. 281–284.

Donovan, Shaun, "Hurricane Sandy Rebuilding Strategy: Helping Communities Prepare for the Impacts of a Changing Climate," in The HUDdle: U.S. Department of Housing and Urban Development's Official Blog, August 19, 2013. As of January 6, 2014:
http://blog.hud.gov/index.php/2013/08/19/hurricane-sandy-rebuilding-strategy-helping-communities-prepare-for-the-impacts-of-a-changing-climate/

Federal Emergency Management Agency, *Hazus: The Federal Emergency Management Agency's (FEMA's) Methodology for Estimating Potential Losses from Disasters*, web page, 2013. As of July 9, 2013: http://www.fema.gov/hazus

Fischbach, Jordan R., David R. Johnson, David S. Ortiz, Benjamin P. Bryant, Matthew Hoover, and Jordan Ostwald, *Coastal Louisiana Risk Assessment Model: Technical Description and 2012 Coastal Master Plan Analysis Results*, Santa Monica, Calif.: RAND Corporation, TR-1259-CPRA, 2012a. As of July 2, 2013: http://www.rand.org/pubs/technical_reports/TR1259.html

Fischbach, Jordan R., David R. Johnson, David S. Ortiz, Benjamin P. Bryant, Matthew Hoover, and Jordan Ostwald, *CLARA Flood Risk Model Supports Louisiana's Coastal Planning*, Santa Monica, Calif.: RAND Corporation, RB-9688-CPRA, 2012b. As of January 13, 2014: http://www.rand.org/pubs/research_briefs/RB9688.html

Godschalk, David R., Adam Rose, Elliott Mittler, Keith Porter, and Carol Taylor West, "Estimating the Value of Foresight: Aggregate Analysis of Natural Hazard Mitigation Benefits and Costs," *Journal of Environmental Planning and Management*, Vol. 52, No. 6, 2009, pp. 739–756.

Grossi, Patricia, and Robert Muir-Wood, *Flood Risk in New Orleans: Implications for Future Management and Insurability*, Newark, Calif.: Risk Management Solutions, Inc., 2006.

Groves, David G., Jordan R. Fischbach, Evan Bloom, Debra Knopman, and Ryan Keefe, *Adapting to a Changing Colorado River: Making Future Water Deliveries More Reliable Through Robust Management Strategies*, Santa Monica, Calif.: RAND Corporation, RR-242-BOR, 2013. As of November 4, 2013: http://www.rand.org/pubs/research_reports/RR242.html

Groves, David G., Jordan R. Fischbach, Debra Knopman, Christopher Sharon, David R. Johnson, David S. Ortiz, Benjamin P. Bryant, Matthew Hoover, and Jordan Ostwald, *Addressing Coastal Vulnerabilities Through Comprehensive Planning: How RAND Supported the Development of Louisiana's Comprehensive Master Plan*, Santa Monica, Calif.: RAND Corporation, RB-9696-CPRA, 2013. As of January 13, 2014: http://www.rand.org/pubs/research_briefs/RB9696.html

Groves, David G., and Robert J. Lempert, "A New Analytic Method for Finding Policy-Relevant Scenarios," *Global Environmental Change Part A: Human & Policy Dimensions*, Vol. 17, No. 1, 2007, pp. 73–85.

Groves, David G., and Christopher Sharon, "Planning Tool to Support Planning the Future of Coastal Louisiana," *Journal of Coastal Research*, No. 67, Special Issue, Summer 2013, pp. 147–161.

Groves, David G., Christopher Sharon, and Debra Knopman, *Planning Tool to Support Louisiana's Decisionmaking on Coastal Protection and Restoration: Technical Description*, Santa Monica, Calif.: RAND Corporation, TR-1266-CPRA, 2012. As of July 2, 2013: http://www.rand.org/pubs/technical_reports/TR1266.html

Hallegatte, Stephane, Colin Green, Robert J. Nicholls, and Jan Corfee-Morlot, "Future Flood Losses in Major Coastal Cities," *Nature Climate Change*, Vol. 3, No. 9, 2013, pp. 802–806.

Healy, Andrew, and Neil Malhotra, "Myopic Voters and Natural Disaster Policy," *American Political Science Review*, Vol. 103, No. 3, 2009, pp. 387–406.

Hurricane Sandy Rebuilding Task Force, *Hurricane Sandy Rebuilding Strategy: Stronger Communities, A Resilient Region*, August 2013. As of October 15, 2013: http://portal.hud.gov/hudportal/documents/huddoc?id=HSRebuildingStrategy.pdf

Intergovernmental Panel on Climate Change, *Climate Change 2013: The Physical Science Basis—Contribution of Working Group I to the Fifth Assessment Report of the Intergovernmental Panel on Climate Change*, Cambridge, UK: Cambridge University Press, 2013.

———, *Managing the Risks of Extreme Events and Disasters to Advance Climate Change Adaptation: A Special Report of Working Groups I and II of the Intergovernmental Panel on Climate Change*, Cambridge, UK: Cambridge University Press, 2012.

Johnson, David R., Jordan R. Fischbach, and David S. Ortiz, "Estimating Surge-Based Flood Risk with the Coastal Louisiana Risk Assessment Model," *Journal of Coastal Research*, No. 67, Special Issue, Summer 2013, pp. 109–126.

Lempert, Robert J., and Myles T. Collins, "Managing the Risk of Uncertain Threshold Responses: Comparison of Robust, Optimum, and Precautionary Approaches," *Risk Analysis: An International Journal*, Vol. 27, No. 4, 2007, pp. 1009–1026.

Lempert, Robert J., and David G. Groves, "Identifying and Evaluating Robust Adaptive Policy Responses to Climate Change for Water Management Agencies in the American West," *Technological Forecasting & Social Change*, Vol. 77, No. 6, 2010, pp. 960–974.

Lempert, Robert J., David G. Groves, Steven W. Popper, and Steven C. Bankes, "A General, Analytic Method for Generating Robust Strategies and Narrative Scenarios," *Management Science*, Vol. 52, No. 4, 2006, pp. 514–528.

Lempert, Robert J., and Steven W. Popper, "High-Performance Government in an Uncertain World," in Robert Klitgaard and Paul C. Light, eds., *High Performance Government: Structure, Leadership, Incentives*, Santa Monica, Calif.: RAND Corporation, MG-256-PRGS, 2005. As of May 7, 2012: http://www.rand.org/pubs/monographs/MG256.html

Lempert, Robert J., Steven W. Popper, and Steven C. Bankes, *Shaping the Next One Hundred Years: New Methods for Quantitative, Long-Term Policy Analysis*, Santa Monica, Calif.: RAND Corporation, MR-1626-RPC, 2003. As of May 4, 2012: http://www.rand.org/pubs/monograph_reports/MR1626.html

Lopez, Ana, Fai Fung, Mark New, Glenn Watts, Alan Weston, and Robert L. Wilby, "From Climate Model Ensembles to Climate Change Impacts and Adaptation: A Case Study of Water Resource Management in the Southwest of England," *Water Resources Research*, Vol. 45, No. 8, August 2009, p. W08419.

Means, Edward, Maryline Laugier, Jennifer Daw, Laurna Kaatz, and Marc Waage, *Decision Support Planning Methods: Incorporating Climate Change Uncertainties into Water Planning*, San Francisco, Calif.: Water Utility Climate Alliance, 2010. As of May 7, 2012: http://www.wucaonline.org/assets/pdf/actions_whitepaper_012110.pdf

Multihazard Mitigation Council, *Natural Hazard Mitigation Saves: An Independent Study to Assess the Future Savings from Mitigation Activities*, Volume 1—Findings, Conclusions, and Recommendations, Washington, D.C.: National Institute of Building Sciences, 2005. As of August 29, 2013: http://www.floods.org/PDF/MMC_Volume1_FindingsConclusionsRecommendations.pdf

National Climatic Data Center, "Billion-Dollar Weather/Climate Disasters, 1980–2013," web page, National Oceanic and Atmospheric Administration, 2012. As of September 30, 2013: http://www.ncdc.noaa.gov/billions/events

National Research Council, *Informing Decisions in a Changing Climate*, Washington, D.C.: The National Academies Press, 2009. As of April 30, 2012: http://www.nap.edu/openbook.php?record_id=12626

NYC Special Initiative for Rebuilding and Resiliency, *PlaNYC: A Stronger, More Resilient New York*, New York, NY: New York City's Office of Long-Term Planning and Sustainability (OLTPS), 2013. As of June 13, 2013: http://www.nyc.gov/html/sirr/html/report/report.shtml

Parris, A., P. Bromirski, V. Burkett, D. Cayan, J. Hall, R. Horton, K. Knuuti, R. Moss, J. Obeysekera, A. Sallenger, and J. Weiss, *Global Sea Level Rise Scenarios for the United States National Climate Assessment*, Silver Spring, Md.: Climate Program Office, NOAA Technical Report OAR CPO-1, December 6, 2012.

Penland, Shea, and Karen E. Ramsey, "Relative Sea-Level Rise in Louisiana and the Gulf of Mexico: 1908-1988," *Coastal Research*, Vol. 6, No. 2, Spring 1990, p. 20.

Pielke, Roger A., and Christopher W. Landsea, "Normalized Hurricane Damages in the United States: 1925–95," *Weather and Forecasting*, Vol. 13, No. 3, 1998, pp. 621–631.

Popper, Steven W., Claude Berrebi, James Griffin, Thomas Light, Endy Y. Min, and Keith Crane, *Natural Gas and Israel's Energy Future: Near-Term Decisions from a Strategic Perspective*, Santa Monica, Calif.: RAND Corporation, MG-927-YSNFF, 2009. As of February 19, 2013: http://www.rand.org/pubs/monographs/MG927.html

RAND Corporation, *RDMlab: Robust Decision Making for Good Decisions Without Predictions*, web page, 2014. As of January 13, 2014:
http://www.rand.org/methods/rdmlab.html

Reed, Denise, and Lee Wilson, "Coast 2050: A New Approach to Restoration of Louisiana Coastal Wetlands," *Physical Geography*, Vol. 25, No. 1, 2004, pp. 4–21.

Schleifstein, Mark, "National Fish and Wildlife Foundation Fund Is Launched to Restore Louisiana, Gulf Coast Natural Resources," *The Times-Picayune*, May 13, 2013. As of September 26, 2013:
http://www.nola.com/environment/index.ssf/2013/05/national_fish_and_wildlife_fou.html

Simon, Herbert A., "Rational Choice and the Structure of the Environment," *Psychological Review*, Vol. 63, No. 2, 1956, pp. 129–138.

U.S. Army Corps of Engineers, "Bonnet Carré Site Selection, Design Advances & Project Statistics," web page, August 29, 2011. As of January 15, 2014:
http://www2.mvn.usace.army.mil/bcarre/designadvances.asp

———, *Louisiana Coastal Protection and Restoration Technical Report*, New Orleans, La.: U.S. Army Corps of Engineers, June, 2009.

Wilbanks, Thomas, *How Geographic Scale Matters in Seeking Community Resilience: Carri Research Report 7*, Oak Ridge, Tenn.: Community and Resilience Research Institute, 2009. As of October 15, 2013:
http://www.resilientus.org/wp-content/uploads/2013/03/T_Wilbanks_CARRI_Report_7_Final_1257273817.pdf